Giant's Stadium, East Rutherford, New Jersey
September 2, 1978

Ever since Gore and the Rock
ent to see the Dead last
ring, I've been achin' to get to a show. All summer
e listen to DEAD/LIVE and I have to hear them **RAVE**.
etter than stacking dishes at the Circle Diner, for sure! In
gust, Gore hears about a Giant's Stadium show. There's
upposed to be one at Cornell, too, and we gotta mail off
r tickets. But Gore gets a note back that says the show
as CANCELLED by the administration.

he Rock drives us to the Meadowlands — I don't have
y license yet and Gore has no car. We get there in the early
afternoon, but we don't go in 'cuz Gore says the Dead won't go on
ntil after dark — that's what happened when he went to
Englishtown last year. We're hanging with two dudes in a
u when one of them rolls down his window for some fresh
air. We hear Friend of the Devil and we think it must be
HE OPENING ACT - New Riders. But when the next
tune is Minglewood Blues, we all take off running
and we get to our seats just in time for the start
of Looks Like Rain. MY FIRST DEAD SONG!

The Dead finish before it gets dark.

— Set I —
Jack Straw
Friend of the Devil
New, New Minglewood Blue
Dicewolf
Looks Like Rain
Stagger Lee
I Need a Miracle
Everyday
Pretty Peggy O'
Lazy Lightning →
Supplication

— Set II —
Good Lovin
Sugar Magnolia
Fire on the Mountain
Estimated Prophet
Eyes of the World
Rhythm Devils
Scarlet Begonias
Sunshine Daydream

— Encore —
One More Saturday Night

The only
live Dead
music we
have is
LIVE/DEAD and
the only decent stereo
is the console in
Katman's basement. So
every day after school
we head down there to
get off and listen to it
straight through. Well, I
didn't Know that Katman
hadn't pnt SIDE 1 & 2 in
the Sleeve. When I grabbed
the album cover to vse it
for picking ont seeds and stems,
the record fell out and oooops—
SHATTERED.

Now all we have is
Dark Star
Death Don't Have No Mercy
Feedback

And We Bid You Goodnight
(Sorry Katman!)

BURBANK, HOME OF WARNER BROS. RECORDS

LIVE/DEAD
THE GRATEFUL DEAD
Produced by The Grateful Dead
And Bob And Betty

SIDE
2

Made in U.S.A.

Warner Communications Company

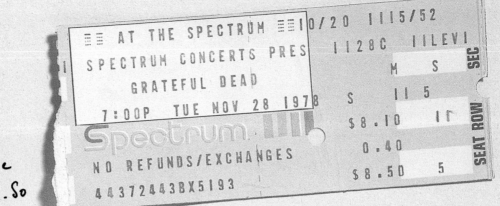

Philly 1/5/79

I'm psyched to see the Dead in
Philly on my birthday, but the
tour gets postponed after the
Cap theater radio show because
Jerry has bronchitis or something. So
the Philly shows are January 5th
and 12th, 1979. Jerry plays Nobody's Fault at the first show and I have to believe him.

My last time seeing them
with Keith and Donna
1/12/79

On the road leading out of Capitol Centre a limo tries to sneak
around all the traffic that's lined up. Screw them! we yell to
the Rock who's behind the wheel. DON'T LET 'EM PASS!
We're laughing and all proud because we cut off the Rich Puick
in the limo until the guy in the lane next to us
rolls down his window and tells us that
it's Weir in the limo. We duck as
the Rock lets him pass so that
Weir won't see our faces.

HAPPY THANKSGIVING!

Long, strange trip #87,935

By CHRIS CLARK

8:07 a.m.—alarm goes off, immediately ingest 50 mg. uncut LSD-25. Go back to sleep before eyes open.

9:46—eyes open because things are getting too intense on the eyelids. Notice that blanket has turned into Cheryl Tiegs, smile, put on *Aoxomoxoa*. Crawl into bathroom, attempt to swim laps in the bathtub. Take 37 bong hits and find a juicy Vantage Light butt under the refrigerator. Forget to light it.

10:22—phone rings, forget which room you left it in. Put on *Workingman's Dead*, find telephone in the aquarium, agree to meet Ron at the Aristocrat in half an hour. Space on hologram-metaphysics, run through "Friend of the Devil" on guitar without a G-string, wonder where you left the mescaline. Smile again. You remember you've got field tickets and were supposed to go over to Folsom when the alarm went off. First wave of panic.

10:58—can't find *Steal Your Face*, now sweating profusely. Bacon turned into green lizards at the 'Crat, had to leave before the little fat men . . . never mind. Roommate is playing the Clash again, where's *Seastones* when you really need it? Find mescaline in backpack, eat it all to counteract acid. Merely complicates geometry of reality. Consumes 47 times its weight in excess. . . wonder if you'll get a guitar pick from Jerry today, decide to wear the *Blues for Allah* jersey. Look for car keys. Take short detour through the Roger Dean mural. The Clash sound like an electric garage door trying to kill democracy. Must run away.

11:30—get halfway before you remember that this concert *isn't* at Red Rocks. Second wave of panic. Opening second pack of cigarettes as you realize you were supposed to pick up Shelia too. *Heaven Help the Fool* jams in the tapedeck, begin having nervous breakdown, swerve to avoid 280-ZX

continued on page 13

FEYLINE Presents
Red Rocks
Summer of Stars
1980

A SUMMER OF STARS

PEPSI

JUNE:

1	MARSHALL TUCKER BAND
9	TOM PETTY
14	RUFUS/BROTHERS JOHNSON
18	KENNY LOGGINS/JOHN STEWART
24-26	DOOBIE BROTHERS
27	LITTLE RIVER BAND/PURE PRAIRIE LEAGUE/ AIR SUPPLY

JULY:

1	JIMMY BUFFETT
2	LEON RUSSELL with NEW GRASS REVIVAL/ JERRY JEFF WALKER/ASLEEP at the WHEEL
5	CHUCK MANGIONE
11	CRYSTAL GAYLE
16	BLUES BROTHERS
29	AL JARREAU/SPYRO GYRA
30	CHEAP TRICK

AUGUST:

2	WAYLON JENNINGS
3	EMMYLOU HARRIS
8-9	THE CARS
11-13	BARRY MANILOW
14	POCO
15-16	REO SPEEDWAGON
17	GEORGE BENSON
26	WILLIE NELSON/BOBBY BARE

SEPTEMBER:

6	A SALUTE TO THE BLUES: B.B. KING/ CLIMAX BLUES BAND
9	BONNIE RAITT

DATES TO BE ANNOUNCED:
KINKS
SANTANA
FIREFALL
ALLMAN BROTHERS
ROBERTA FLACK/PEABO BRYSON
ALICE COOPER
BEACH BOYS
AMERICA
JOURNEY

Feyline

15th Anniversary

Folsom Field, University of Colorado
Boulder, Colorado   June 7 ÷ 8, 1980

We left at 10 p.m. on June 3, 1980, ← an hour after the last final of my freshman year at Rider!

drove all night and all day. We stopped at a Best Western in Blue Springs, Missouri on 6/4.

The next afternoon we almost lost the Rabbit's driver-side door to the tailwind of a semi flying by on a highway in Kansas, but fortunately the Rock holds onto the door, and it's just bent outta shape.

6/7/80
—Set I—
Jack Straw
Friend of the Devil
 El Paso
 Mama Tried
 Ramblin' Rose
Passenger
Far From Me
All, All, All, New
New, New Minglewood
 Blues
Loser
Feel Like A Stranger
 Deal

— SET II —
Bertha →
Greatest Story Ever Told
Althea
Lost Sailor →
Saint of Circumstance →
 Drums →
 Not Fade Away →
 Wharf Rat →
Good Lovin' →

—Encores—

6/8/80
—Set I—
Uncle John's Band →
 Playing in the Band →
Me And My Uncle
 Mexicali Blues
Tennessee Jed
Samson ÷ Delilah
Easy To Love You
 Althea
Looks Like Rain
 Deal

— SET II —
Feel Like A Stranger
 Ship of Fools
Estimated Prophet →
Eyes of the World →
 Drums →
Saints of Circumstance
 Black Peter →
Sugar Magnolia
—Encores—
Alabama Getaway-
Brokedown Palace

Alabama Getaway → One More Saturday Night / U.S. Blues

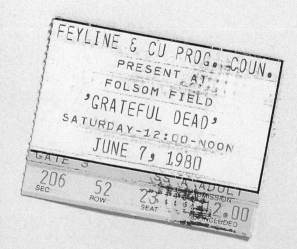

Gene and I knew lots of people from Monmouth County that were hitting the midwest stops on the summer '81 tour. We were certain we would hook up with one of them in St. Paul. We were so certain that we bought one-way tickets to fly out. But an hour before showtime, we hadn't seen anyone we knew. We decided to get a ride to Alpine Valley for the next night's gig. ~~~~ with anyone who would take us. And then JB walked up. He was a chatty but odd dude from Milwaukee and he had come to St. Paul alone. He'd be happy to take us to East Troy — he knew just where he was going. So we stowed our packs in his car and went to see what turned out to be a cookin' show at the St. Paul Civic Center.

When we met up with JB after the show, he introduced us to Fry and Cat, a couple from Brooklyn. Now we were a crew, driving across Minnesota and Wisconsin. We stopped at a rest area and learned all about sphagnum moss. John walked up to a light swarming with moths and bugs — and stood calmly as they flew into his bushy hair and beard. He pulled them out one by one as we drove on. We also learned that Fry and Cat didn't eat meat, but plenty of chemicals. We arrived in Milwaukee around 7 a.m. We had no place to go, so JB took us to the zoo. Then he continued our cultural tour through the Heileman's brewery. The sour smell made me kind of queasy — it was about 10:30 am but I drank a few free cups anyway.

We killed the early afternoon hanging in a city park. Later, JB took us to a pre-concert party at a friend's house, who didn't hide that he was pissed at JB for showing up with a crew of well-burnt 'Heads. We convinced JB to leave soon and finally got to Alpine Valley. We parted from the crew to look for a ride back to New Jersey. Which we never found and we ended up buying bus tickets home from Gary, Indiana. How we got there is another story...

4/15/82

Bruz wore these jeans to every show, night after night, indoors and out.
Like he's superstitious or something. They're cool, for sure, with a bandanna patch
on the knee. At the first note of Morning Dew, he jumps and we all
hear a big **RIP.** I think everybody in Rhode Island heard that rip.
Except Bruz. He's dancing so crazy, his ass hanging out, and if he's noticed
that his pants are wide open, he's doing a great job hiding it. After the show
he's freezing. And as we drop him off at 4:15 a.m. at his
house, we finish the job that Dew started.

One of these scoundrels kidnapped an innocent little lawn ornament as they left town for a summer road trip. The blindfolded the bunny and everywhere the went they took his picture, so his owners would see what a good time he had when he returned.

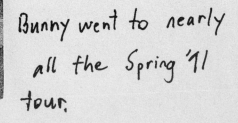

Bunny went to nearly all the Spring '91 tour.

After/ gracious taught Tuna and me how to make "tie weaves". We spent most of summer making them while we listened to tapes. No reason—just something to do and a lot more creative than internity in the "art" department at the ad agency where my dad works. When we got tickets to see Rich Stadium on July 4, 1986, we decided to sell our summer's work at the show. We rode up in the back of our buddy Bobbin's truck.

About 3 miles from the stadium, traffic comes to a dead halt. Tuna and me hop out and start selling our strings. We had 100. For the next 4 hours, we walked from car to ~~bus~~ to van to bus, talking with everyone we met. We sold as strings for $1 apiece, and we were really psyched.

Except we totally lost Bobbin and his truck—which is where our tickets were. So we walked to the gate hoping for a Miracle. And there was Bobbin, in line, just getting ready to go in. We screamed and hugged he asked. "What the hell happened to you guys?!" We ran back to the truck to get our tickets and got inside just as the 1st set ended.

I Need A Miracle Every Day—

Some Kind of Miracle

Bunny must have enjoyed the trip, because he never made a peep! And when he was restored to his rightful place at home, his owners put up a sign: "Hurray, Our Bunny is Back!"

pangler Jay Spangler, Mr. Moderation, got fried last night. Maybe it was the
rand new crescent moon, maybe it was "St. Stephen", maybe it was the sweet
acey blond sitting on his right, or maybe it was the 2 very generous dudes
beside her, who seemed to have a
limitless supply of everything.

whatever the reason, Spangler
Jay Spangler was too far gone
to drive his precious Super
Beetle home from Long Island

I got the hang of driving
a stick within a couple of laps
around the Nassau parking lot.
And except for a stall out or two
at the toll booths and a few grinds
from ~~second~~ third to
second instead of fourth, I did pretty well.

And Spangler Jay Spangler had the clutch replaced in no time.

FUKENGRUVEN

LIFE ON THE REBOUND

by R. Yodes

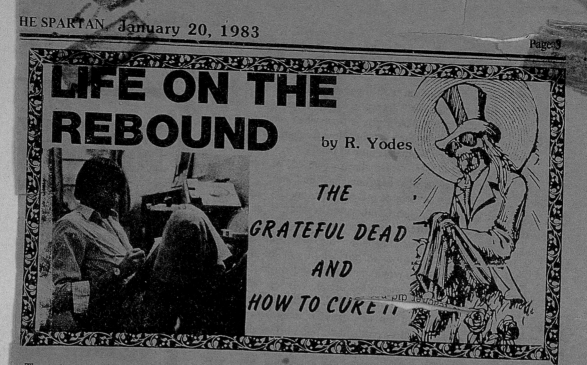

THE GRATEFUL DEAD AND HOW TO CURE IT

There is a horrible disease in America known as the Grateful Dead. When this dease manifests itself in human beings, the victim is refered to as a "Deadhead." The first symptom of the illness is usually a public announcement, proclaiming that out of the many types of music available, and the thousands of musical performers on this planet, the Grateful Dead are the closest thing to perfection that we will find in this life.

Other symptoms often seen in deadheads are a need to wear faded denim clothing. This clothing is usually worn in tandem with various dead-artifacts that include T-shirts, buttons, patches, hankerchiefs, underwear, etc. . . . It is thus equipped that most deadheads hit the road to try seeing the object of their obsession performing in concert.

Grateful Dead shows are different from most concerts, there is a great deal of audience response, dancing, and fellowship. A person infected with the Grateful Dead however, often takes it way to far. In many cases Deadheads will use their last remainders of time, money and sanity to follow the Grateful Dead concert tours. This odessy may last for many weeks through several states until final reserves, both physical and mental, are exhausted. There is an old saying that often proves true, "Deadheads don't have jobs - they go on tour."

If you have a loved one who has fallen into the monotonous rut of constantly playing Grateful Dead music, it is possible that you can save him. One thing that must be kept in mind is that you cannot directly tell a deadhead that his obsession over one band is totally pathetic. You must neverforget that deadheads usually believe that if you have any taste in music, the only way you could not love the Dead, it to not know them well enough.

There are ways to gradually deprogram your deadhead. One thing you can do is play music to him by musicians like Little Feat, the Dixie Dregs, and Neil Young. Exposure to such bands with similar styles of Country-- Rock-Blues may show him that there is a possibility other bands can do some of the things the Dead do, may be even better.

Many Deadheads have a need to own dozens of cassette recordings (bootlegs) from live Dead concerts. A deadhead gains as much enjoyment from his 27th live Jerry Garcia guitar solo recording, as he did his first. Someday a deadhead you know may come to you excited with a sparkle in his eye, and an obscure 10 year old Dead recording in his hand. When he does, try to restrain yourself for a moment then ask your friend to honestly comment on the quality of the recording. If the tape is typical of a Grateful Dead bootleg, it is a recording of a recording of a recording of a concert made in the midst of a screaming crowd, on a midget tape recorder, smuggled in under a girl's long gypsy dress. If your friend doesn't admit that the recording is of inferior quality, he probably cannot hear well, and it's no wonder he became a deadhead.

When your friend tries to tell you that the Grateful Dead's music is fantastically deep, complex, and perfect; dont take it lying down. Point out to your friend that there are lots of younger musicians 12 and 13 years old, who can play many of the Dead's more popular songs. Much of this ability is not because the children are that talented, but because the music is, for the most part, fairly simple. Gently remind your deadhead that just because Bob Weir can get through the same songs that he's played the last 15 years, doesn't make him the greatest rhythm guitarist that ever experienced flash backs.

Remember that moderate doses of Grateful Dead music is not dangerous in itself. It is only when the music listener becomes obsessed with the Dead, and the Dead lifestyle that the music listener is in danger of stagnation between the ears. It may even be possible that someday scientists will finish researching their theories on positive uses for the Grateful Dead's music, a subsitute for some forms of electro-shock theraphy.

50!

- 9/2/78 Giant's Stadium
X 11/21/78 Rochester, NY
11/23/78 Landover, MD
X 1/5/79 Phila. Spectrum
X 1/7/79 Madison Square Garden
X 1/10/79 Nassau Colliseum
• 1/12/79 Phila. Spectrum
- 1/17/79 New Haven C.C.
X 1/18/79 Providence C.C.
• 5/4/79 Hampton Roads
X 5/5/79 Baltimore C.C.
5/7/79 Lafayette College, PA
5/8/79 Penn State
• 5/11/79 Billorica, MA
X 5/12/79 UMass
X 5/13/79 Portland, Maine
X 8/31/79 Glens Falls, NY
• 9/1/79 Holleder Stadium, Rochester
• 9/5/79 Madison Square Garden
X 9/6/79 MSG
• 10/31/79 Nassau
X 11/5/79 Phila Spectrum
- 11/6/79 Spectrum
X 11/30/79 Stanley Theater, Pittsburgh
X 12/1/79 Stanley Theater
X 3/3/80 Capital Theater, Passaic, NJ
• 5/10/80 Hartford C.C.
X 5/15/80 Nassau

X 5/16/80 Nassau
• 6/7/80 Folsom Field, University
X 6/8/80 of Colorado, Boulder
• 8/29/80 Phila. Spectrum
X 8/30/80 Spectrum
• 10/25/80 ⎤ RADIO CITY
X 10/29/80 ⎟ MUSIC HALL
X 10/31/80 ⎦ NEW YORK, NY
• 3/7/80 University of MD.
• 3/10/81 MSG
3/14/81 Hartford C.C.
• 5/2/81 Phila. Spectrum
5/4/81 Spectrum
• 5/9/81 Nassau
X 5/13/81 Providence C.C.
X 5/15/81 Rutgers, NJ
X 5/16/81 Cornell University, Ithaca
• 7/10/81 St. Paul, Minnesota
• 7/11/81 Alpine Valley Music Theater
East Troy, WI
9/25/81 Lehigh University, PA
X 9/26/81 Buffalo, NY
9/27/81 Landover, MD

Lindsay and me took my punky brother to his very first show at the Sam Boyd Stadium in Vegas. We left him at our seats when we went off to search for water. By the time we got back, he's nowhere to be found. We scan the crowd looking for him and we finally spot him — just a few feet from the stage dancing like a madman, his shirt tied around his waist.

WPLJ RADIO ROCKS THE MEADOWLANDS WITH

GRATEFUL DEAD

APRIL 16, 17, 1983

WPLJ 95.5
THE HOME OF ROCK 'N ROLL

WPLJ 95.5
THE HOME OF ROCK 'N ROLL

The WPLJ
Rock 'n Roll
Bandanna.
$3.00
Available in
assorted colors.

Send check
or money
order to:
WPLJ Bandanna,
Box 1395,
New York, N.Y.
10101.

HONORARY
JERRY GARCIA BAND
MEMBER
DEADICATED
DEADHEAD
MEMBER OFFICIAL SINCE '65

stereo broadcasts, bringing their reputation for live performance to a wider audience than could be accommodated in the smaller, more intimate halls. Their second live double-album *Grateful Dead* (1971) was recorded in conjunction with those broadcasts. Keith Godchaux joined the band in 1971 as pianist, and Donna Godchaux as

female vocalist in 1973, and they remained with the band until 1979.

In 1972 the Dead traveled by bus in Europe for two months, played and recorded in seven countries, came home and released a triple live album *Europe '72*. Later that year Pigpen died following a series of operations for stomach and liver

ailments.

In 1973 and 1974 the Dead's growing popularity faced them and their organization with the need to design and build a concert system capable of high quality sound reproduction on a large scale, in order to play in arenas and stadiums. With the addition of digital-delay sound towers at open-air

concerts, the Dead were also able to play to large summer audiences, such as Watkins Glen, with a record attendance of 600,000 people, where they played with The Band and The Allman Brothers. They also took this system on a second European Tour in 1974.

On completion of their Warner Bros. recor-

Some folks trust to reason
    Others trust to might
        I don't trust to nothin'
            But I know it come out right.

ATLANTA GOLD PRINTS - AWARD WINNING PHOTOGRAPHY

Greetings from Six Flags over Georgia! Truly an exciting adventure every time you visit. Young and old should not miss a visit to the park, especially at night when fire-crackers truly make it "Hot-Lanta!"

Dear Eric,
Miss. ½ step
Walking Blues
Built to Last *   Scarlet
We Can Run But   Fire
We Can't Hide **   Estimated
Gween Jane Approx.   Eyes
Candyman   Drums
Cassidy   Space
Touch of Grey   The Wheel
                        I Need A Miracle
* Jerry   Standing on the Moon *
** Brent   Lovelight
                        U.S. Blues.
Love + Kisses, Me.

Pub. by Aerial Photography Services, Inc. 5859 N. Peachtree Rd., Atlanta, Ga. 30340
© Aerial Photography Services, Inc.

APS

Post Card

N.B. Meyer
_____ 27th st

Goin' Where
Don't Blow

HORN CO. GLENSIDE, PA 19038

Who is the North American
Skanking Society? Where do they march?
Why are they so skanking?

Greetings from
ATLANTA, GEORGIA
The metropolitan capital of the South. An aerial
panoramic view of the city with the Omni Sports
Complex in the center.

Dear Eric,

Let the Good Times Roll   Samson & Delilah
Franklin's Tower →   Ship of Fools
Feel Like a Stranger   Playing in the Band
Stagger Lee   Foolish Heart
— Memphis Blues Again   D/S
Ramble on Rose   Gimme Some Lovin
Let it Grow   Wharf Rat
Dough Knees.   Throwing Stones
                            NFA
Dan says
H I gh   Box of Rain.

GA Scenic South Co., Box 14, Pell City, AL 35125

POST CARD

Eric "Peritz" Meyer
SW 97th St.

Somebody goes to Atlanta and
all I get is a
couple of
postcards with
set lists.

Some buddy!

Be Wind
Strange

Halloween at
Rockefeller Center

NEW
DEAD
GARD

we had to park the '70 Nova in a garage where they park for you. After the sh...
the guy comes back without the car but an apologetic look on his face. The Nova's
clutch won't work. My brother doesn't know what to do; the guy leads us to the
furthest, darkest corner of the garage. While my brother's head is under the hood, I spot

JERSEY

⚡ HEAD

EN STATE

↑↑ These photos are out of order but I don't have room for them anywhere else. Familiar faces and blurred memories. Never had such a good time in my life before, I'd like to have it one more time.....

something moving out of the corner of my eyes I may have been hallucinating, but I wasn't seeing things. A rat. A big-ass rat. I keep a watch out for it, but I don't tell my brother so he won't get freaked (like I am) to finish the job. I think they were closing in when we left.

WELCOME TO
"JERRY GARCIA ON BROADWAY"
AT THE
LUNT-FONTANNE THEATRE

Much effort has gone into creating an environment that suits all of us; our gratitude to the people who loaned us the memorabilia in the lobby, and to all the personnel that helped to put this event together.

The Lunt-Fontanne is a theatre with seats, yet we know that many of you are gonna want to stretch and boogie — so, under the circumstances, and out of respect for the people around you, we ask you to avail yourself of the outer lobby areas when the bug bites. We'll have speakers in the lobbies, so the music will follow you. In return, we ask you please to refrain from standing on the seats and moving out into the aisles. This means a great deal to us, and we appreciate your cooperation.

Enjoy!

Cheers!
Bill

p.s.: Reminder: **NO SMOKING — NO TAPING**

As my brother and I were driving away from the theater, a limo pulled up next to us. I looked over and saw Jerry light a cigarette in the back seat. As the limo sped up, I yelled, "Stay with it!" We drove uptown alongside the limo, jumping a couple yellow lights hoping for a glimpse. We both stopped at a red light — Jerry dropped his window and gave us the thumbs up. The light changed, the limo turned onto a side street, and we were lost. Totally lost.

And now kids, the Cartoon that broke the mold. No, not Doonesbury®, not Calvin & Hobbes®,
Cosmic Irrelevance
Dateline: 7/10/87 JFK Phila, Pa.
Scene #1
Wow, great drums! Mickey & Billy are Really on tonight.
Yeah & Let's go get Something to Drink before the "End of Space"
Scene #2
Excuse me, are the Grateful Dead still on Stage?
They're in "Space".
LIMIT BEERS NK
END OF SPACE
DRI
WARM Disgusting BEVERAGE
Blue Chiffon
Scene #3
If I have to explain, you wouldn't understand...
?!!?
Did you hear what that guy Just told me?
Pink Taffetta
Tune in Next time kids when we answer the question: Why was it holding the mold in the first place?

Jones has to be either the luckiest or unluckiest guy ever. I can't decide.
He'd been living out in Berkeley for a year when he came back for the summer '84
tour. He didn't call any of us — figured we'd just all hook up on tour.
He didn't see anyone he knew in Harrisburg, PA, so he hitched a ride up to
Saratoga Springs with three guys in a Toyota. On the way, the pulled off the road to
catch some ZZzz's. Jones was too cramped to sleep in the back seat, so he pulled
out his pack and left to lie in the grass. When he woke up the Toyota was gone.

Jones grabbed a ride ~~up to~~
almost right away in a VW that couldn't go faster
than 25 mph. Highway Patrol pulled them over and
found a shotgun under the front seat and a
bag of mushrooms on the other passenger.

The local judge, in his bathrobe
fines Jones the contents of
his wallet for hitching.

Selling these patches sure seemed like an easy and fr

Back on the road, Jones gets a
ride from a Ryder truck crammed with abou
25 Deadheads, including a girl who
had just been freed from a body
cast she'd had on for a year.

She takes a liking to our man,
and when the truck stops at
the lake resort, they sneak
off into the bushes.

Meanwhile, the driver of the truck
gets busted at the lake, and the
Heads disperse. So Jones and the
girl walk to the nearest highway
To catch a ride. Which they do...
with 3 guys in a Toyota.

ray to meet people and make a little cash. And it was for

the first 45 minutes...

Every room at the Red Roof Inn in Noblesville, Indiana
looked lit up by the time Larissa and I got back to our
room after the second Deer Creek show. A guy wearing
nothing but a pair of shorts was in the hallway across
from our room, holding two buckets of ice. He invited
us to a party in his room at the other end of the hall. The
ice in his hands and the glaze in his eyes suggested the
was already in full swing.

    In his room, the beds were pushed together all the way
against the wall and a dozen or so people were dancing with no one in particular
and making regular trips to the bathroom to refill their cups with beer from
the keg in the tub. We danced awhile but we were tired from the show,
so we went to see what was going on in the adjoining room, where the
door was slightly ajar. We peeked inside. The music was blasting so loud
it was distorted to the point of being painful. Five or six people were in
there with a tank of nitrous oxide in the middle of the room. A few
were staggering around with balloons and puffed-out cheeks. Some were
doubled over in silent, convulsive laughter. One guy was just lying on his
back strumming his air guitar, oblivious to the
people stepping over him. We turned and went to
check out the other adjoining room.

Its door was closed but we saw a few people coming and going, and it seemed a lot more mellow. When we looked in the room it was hazy with incense and we heard the sounds of Mickey and Billy thrumming through their collection of percussion instruments and listening to the drummers on tape. When our eyes adjusted to the low lights, all we could see was a lot of flesh splayed out all over the floor and beds. Larissa and I had just met on the spring tour and weren't ready for that scene, so we passed on that room and went back to dancing.

My first
bootleg tape!

My computerized
tape list. The first
guy I send it to,
Mulvey, sends me 3
cases of blanks and
detailed instructions on
how to set the levels for
his tapes

FLOOR
SEC ROW SEAT
107 3 14
ADMIT ONE THIS DATE ONLY
ELECTRIC FACTORY Presents
GRATEFUL DEAD
AT THE SPECTRUM IN PHILADELPHIA, PA OCT. 18, 1989 WED.—7:30 PM
PLEASE: NO CANS, BOTTLES, ALCOHOL, PETS OR VIDEO EQUIPMENT OF ANY KIND. NO CAMPING OR VENDING
TAPER
FLOOR SECTION
T 16
GDEAD
20.00
JOHN SCHER PRESENTS
GRATEFUL DEAD
* * *
TAPER
MEADOWLANDS ARENA
EAST RUTHERFORD, NJ
MON OCT 16, 1989 7:30PM
ROW/BOX S SEAT 15
SECTION
PRICE GDEAD 20.00
JOHN SCHER PRESENTS
GRATEFUL DEAD
* * *
TAPER
MEADOWLANDS ARENA
FLOOR
SEC ROW SEAT
107 14 8
ADMIT ONE THIS DATE ONLY
ELECTRIC FACTORY Presents
GRATEFUL DEAD
TAPER
AT THE SPECTRUM IN PHILADELPHIA, PA OCT. 19, 1989 THUR.—7:30 PM
PLEASE: NO CANS, BOTTLES, ALCOHOL, PETS OR VIDEO EQUIPMENT OF ANY KIND. NO CAMPING OR VENDING
TWR-C/GATE-8
SEC ROW SEAT
56D B 12
LOGE/TAPER
ADMIT ONE THIS DATE ONLY
JOHN SCHER Presents
GRATEFUL DEAD
MADISON SQUARE GARDEN NEW YORK CITY SEPT. 20, 1990 THUR.—7:30 PM
Please: No Cans, Bottles, Alcohol, Flash Cameras or Video Equipment of ANY Kind.
2
U 8
FLOOR SECTION
ADULT
17.50
JOHN SCHER PRESENTS
GRATEFUL DEAD
** TAPER
MEADOWLANDS ARENA
EAST RUTHERFORD, NJ
1987 7:30PM
2
ROW/BOX S SEAT 9
FLOOR SECTION
PRICE GDEAD 20.00
JOHN SCHER PRESENTS
GRATEFUL DEAD
* * *
TAPER
MEADOWLANDS ARENA
EAST RUTHERFORD, NJ
7:30PM
PORTAL 48
SEC ROW SEAT
128F HH 2
LOWER/TAPER
ADMIT ONE THIS DATE ONLY
CELLAR DOOR Presents
Grateful Dead
THE OMNI ATLANTA, GA
MARCH 20, 1993 SATURDAY • 7:30 PM
NO CAMPING, OVERNIGHT PARKING
2
V 5
FLOOR SECTION
PRICE GDEAD 20.00
JOHN SCHER PRESENTS
GRATEFUL DEAD
* * *
TAPER
MEADOWLANDS ARENA
EAST RUTHERFORD, NJ
SUN OCT 15, 1989 8:30PM

FRETS

JUL. '85

JERRY GARCIA

On Soloing, Bluegrass, And The Grateful Dead

13 Incredible BANJO ROLLS

Crosspicking by MARK O'CONNOR

Texas Playboy's Fiddler KEITH COLEMAN

GRATEFUL DEAD

LIVE IN CONCERT
Sunday, October 8 & Monday, October 9, 1989
BOTH SHOWS SOLD OUT — NO TICKETS AVAILABLE
IF YOU DO NOT HAVE A TICKET, YOU WILL NOT BE ALLOWED IN THE PARKING LOT.

To all Grateful Dead fans who will be attending one or both of the shows at the Hampton Coliseum, we would like to welcome you to our facility. For all fans who are not from the Hampton Roads area attending the shows, we would like to assist you in making your visit to Hampton a pleasant experience.

In order to facilitate your visit to the Coliseum, we are providing ~~following information for your convenience~~ and understanding.

CONCERT INFORMATION

1. All shows will begin at 7:30 p.m.
2. Doors will open early enough for everyone ~~ample opportunity for entry before sho~~
3. Audio taping will only be permitted ~~designated area behind the sou~~ ~~location is limited and is a~~ ~~first serve basis. Once t~~ ~~tape decks will be allow~~ ~~tape in a different sectio~~ ~~leave. Video taping will n~~
4. Backpacks, knapsacks, etc.

~~eum. Therefore, it is advisable to store these~~ ~~elsewhere before you enter the building.~~ ~~d has requested that we ask you to please~~ ~~thing that might jeopardize their ability~~ ~~mpton Coliseum in the future.~~ ~~emember, you are responsible for your~~ ~~actions!~~

We understand that you want to stand and dance and enjoy the show, but please try to keep the aisles clear so that we can keep with the Fire Department regulations.

PARKING INFORMA~~TION~~

1. All parking lots will be va~~ concert.~~ Once the lots have been ~~c~~ ~~ll be~~ reopened at 12:00 noon the ~~ing day.~~
2. There will be personnel ar~~ these areas to~~ assist you with any questions you may have regarding camping, parking or lodging.

3. Portable restroom facilities are provided at the Coliseum. Please ask parking personnel for directions.
4. Absolutely no vending or overnight camping will be permitted on these premises!!
5. NO open flame, cooking, etc.

BEWARE OF COUNTERFEIT TICKETS—Tickets will be checked carefully at the door for counterfeits.
All tickets should have been purchased from legitimate Ticket Outlets.*
*WE CANNOT BE RESPONSIBLE FOR LOSSES DUE TO PURCHASE OF COUNTERFEIT TICKETS.

VIRGINIA STATE LAW

The Virginia State Law prohibits the drinking of alcoholic beverages in public. It is illegal to consume alcoholic beverages in this parking lot whether in your vehicle or not, or inside the Coliseum. Uniformed and non-uniformed police officers will patrol the lot and Coliseum to ensure that all laws are obeyed. Also, **the following items are not allowed on the premises:**

Alcoholic Beverages	Glass or metal containers	Knives or Weapons of any type
Illegal Drugs or Controlled Substances	Fireworks or incendiary devices	Frisbees in the Coliseum

or any packages, parcels or items (the contents of which are not displayed).

To ensure public safety, you may be requested to display the contents or nature of any package, parcel or item in your posession.

You do not have to comply with the request to display the contents of any package, parcel or item. Instead, you may return the item to your vehicle or surrender it at the checkpoint before you are permitted entrance to the Coliseum.

MEDICAL ASSISTANCE
Hospitals / Emergency Centers
1. Hampton General, 3120 Victoria Blvd., Hampton . . . 727-7000
2. Newport News General
   5100 Marshall Ave., Newport News 247-7200
3. Norfolk General, 600 Gresham Dr., Norfolk 628-3000
4. DePaul, 150 Kingsley Lane, Norfolk 489-5000
5. Hope Center, 300 Marcella Rd., Hampton 727-7456
6. Minor Emergency Center
   2148 W. Mercury Blvd., Hampton. 827-1940
7. Secure Urgent Care
   1326 E. Little Creek Rd., Norfolk. 583-0404

Drug Abuse Centers
1. Peninsula Hosp., 2242 Executive Dr., Hampton 827-1001
2. Riverside Hospital
   420 J. Clyde Morris Blvd., Newport News 599-2000
3. Norfolk Drug Treatment
   2811-C Lafayette Blvd., Norfolk. 857-1155

FOOD AND BEVERAGE INFORMATION

1. There are a number of restaurants located across from the Coliseum and in the Coliseum Mall.

2. 24-hour Restaurants:

   Denny's, 1040 W. Mercury Blvd., Hampton
   Daybreak, (Day's Inn), 1918 Coliseum Drive, Hampton
   Hardee's 908 Big Bethel Road, Hampton
   Hardee's 63 W. Mercury Blvd., Hampton
   International House of Pancakes, 1002 W. Mercury Blvd., Hampton
   McDonald's, 1311 W. Mercury Blvd., Hampton
   Omelet Shoppe, 1811 W. Mercury Blvd., Hampton
   Shoney's, 1527 W. Pembroke Ave., Newport News
   Steak 'n Egg Kitchen, 10312 Jefferson Ave., Newport News
   Waffle House, 2600 W. Mercury Blvd., Hampton
   Wendy's, 1024 W. Mercury Blvd., Hampton

~~LLAR DOOR PRESENT~~
~~MERLY~~
arlock~~s~~
~~N COLISEUM~~
~~OBER 9, 1989 - 7:30 P.M.~~
~~UNDS / NO EXCHANGES~~
~~OHOL OR VIDEO EQUIPMENT OF ANY KIND.~~
~~CAMPING OR VENDING~~

$18.50
MONDAY 7:30 P.M.
OCTOBER 9, 1989
Weldon Williams & Lick, Inc.
TKT. GEN.
NO . 74749
ADM.

Thur. 18th	Vegas
9:30	Gabey + Heather
11:05	Nat + Jeff USAIR Philly
11:25	Bob Continental #761 cleveland (Gate) Michael Ferr
11:43	Big Steve + Jean America West #742
11:49	Royce + Denise = United # 629 Chicago Meet baggage or outside

3575 Vegas Blvd Flamingo Hilton (Grand Vacation Resort) 702 697-2900 Keller

FRI. 19th	Dave: N.W. 1191 (Detroit) Leave D.C. 7 AM 10:37

P/up in front of baggage claim HM 703-532-3880 OR He wi 1-800-444 limo Call San

CAll
AARON !! 2/4/1 FRI. Aftershow

San Tropez
Rm. under Asher ?
Thur. — MON. nite

Dr. Legate

Briggs: Cor 30
HM. 30
D
SA
Big Steve 975   2305

DEAD IN VEGAS
WHAT A LONG STRANGE GAMBLE IT'S BEEN.
May 14, 15, 16

Not DEAD Yet

Rock legends inspire a second wave of improvisational bands

Jim Laurie/Review-Journal

The Dave Matthews Band, below, doesn't sound much like the Grateful Dead, left, the godfathers of psychedelic rock. Yet Matthews, who opens three Sam Boyd Stadium shows for the Dead this weekend, is at the front of a new wave of rootsy, improvisational rockers.

4158

SEC ROW SEAT

GEN. ADM.
MAY 15, 1993

ADMIT ONE THIS DATE ONLY

BILL GRAHAM PRESENTS with
EVENING STAR PRODUCTIONS

Grateful Dead

With Special Guest STING

UNLV SILVER BOWL
UNIV. OF NEVADA, LAS VEGAS

MAY 16, 1993-2 PM

BILL GRAHAM PRESENTS WITH EVENING STAR PRODUCTIONS

GRATEFUL DEAD®

WITH SPECIAL GUEST
"TRAFFIC"

UNLV Silver Bowl · Univ. of Nevada, Las Vegas

Sun., June 26, 1994 · 6:00 P.M. · $30.00

PLEASE: NO CANS, GLASS CONTAINERS, ALCOHOL.
FLASH CAMERAS OR VIDEO EQUIPMENT OF ANY KIND.
(PRICE INCLUDES $1.50 PARKING FEE)

No Vending,

GENERAL ADMISSION   TKT. NO. 78

BILL GRAHAM PRESENTS WITH EVENING STAR PRODUCTIONS

GRATEFUL DEAD

WITH SPECIAL GUEST

UNLV SILVER BOWL · University of Nevada, Las Vegas

Sun., May 21, 1995 · 2:00 PM · $30.00
PLEASE: NO CANS, GLASS CON
FLASH CAMERAS OR VIDEO EQUI
(PRICE INCLUDES $1.50

No Vending, Camping or
No Refund No Exchange - A

GENERAL ADMISSI   TKT. NO.

Sun., May 21, 1995 - 2:00 PM   NO. 3245

Fri., June 24, 1994-6:00PM

BILL GRAHAM PRESENTS WITH EVENING STAR PRODUCTIONS

GRATEFUL DEAD

WITH

ADMIT ONE THIS DATE

Weldon, Williams & Lick

Bass TICKETS
CELEBRATING 20 YEARS OF COMMUNITY SERVICE
1974 · 1994

BILL GRAHAM PR

Weldon, Williams & Lick

05-2:00PM   Sat., June 25, 1994 - 6:00 PM

BILL GRAHAM PRES

ADMIT ONE THIS DATE

---

514 GA FRI GEN ADM

Camping or Overnight Parking

582

EVENING STAR/BGP PRESENTS

<1> GRATEFUL DEAD <1>
/ STING */*

SAM BOYD SILVER BOWL

RAIN OR SHINE/PARKING INC

FRI MAY 14, 1993 2:00PM

ADULT   EVS0514

$ 22.00

GA

EVENT CODE   GA   GEN ADM
SECTION/AISLE   ROW/BOX   SEAT
GEN 17
PHONE
GA FR
L20MAY5

PRESENTS With
STAR PRODUCTIONS
Grateful Dead
Special Guest STING

EVENT CODE   GA   GEN ADM
$ 22.00   SECTION/AISLE   ROW/BOX   SEAT   L-DOS
$ 4.00   ADMISSION

KKLZ 96.3+MOLSON WELCOMES

RADIATORS & HOT TUNA
AT THE LAS VEGAS FISH FRY
DOORS OPEN AT 10:00PM
THE ALADDIN THEATRE
SAT MAY 20, 1995 10:30PM

CALL-FOR-TIX
702-474-4000

NO REFUND
NO EXCHANGE

Ash always lashed a stuffed Felix the Cat

 his microphone stand in the taper's pit,

o that everyone he knew could find him

n the forest of mic stands. As he

d his girlfriend are carrying

their gear back to their car

after a Deer Creek show,

e stops to fix her shoe

nd unknowingly dropped Felix.

mmed, they continued on their tour without

eir mascot.

As they were walking into the show at

entura fairgrounds a few weeks later, Ash spotted Felix

strapped to a car antennae with a note that read, "I'm lost — please

help me find my family."

Ash turned to the owner of the car to tell him that he'd lost

Felix and found himself looking into a familiar face.

It was Bobby Brady, or really Mike Lookinland, who was

happy to return Felix to his rightful owner.

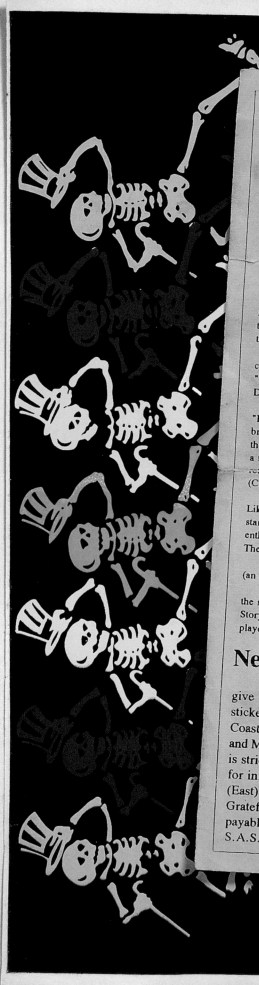

Summer Tour News

Brought to you by the folks at Unbroken Chain

CHARLOTTE REVIEW
by August West

RFK Handout 7/14/91

The boys proved once again this week that they can cook in the South and especially in North Carolina. Greensboro was hot two months ago and Charlotte was even hotter Tuesday and Wednesday.

Hold onto your fanny packs for this!

In the show before tonight's RFK stand, the boys gave us "Desolation Row," "Loose Lucy" and the East Coast's first "C.C. Rider" since 1987 (4/3/87 Worcester). Jerry passed up on his chance for a repeat of Shoreline's "Train to Cry" pairing with "C.C. Rider."

The second set was the Jerry Garcia show, from an energetic "Touch" through a powerful "Saint" to a historic "Women". Jerry's MIDI horn effect on the "Women" jam stole the song and Bobby actually backed away from singing for awhile to give the Fat Man room to pick his way through a treasure trove of musical delights. It was during this Jerry-dominated section of "Women" that Dan Healy decided to crank the volume another notch.

That was good anticipation born of a quarter century of reading the band because the fun continued after drums/space with a fast-clipped "Goin' Down the Road Feeling Bad," a solid "Watchtower" and a mind-numbingly triumphant "Morning Dew." I don't know about you but this Deadhead rode Jerry's guitar strings all the way to Heaven on Wednesday night.

Oh, Tuesday wasn't bad either. "Ike" to open, good solid first set with a searing "Promised Land" to close. There's definitely some sort of chemistry that mixes together into a fine brew in Carolina with Chuck Berry and the Dead. They kept winding up "Promised Land" until they reached warp speed. Hearing that song brought back memories of last July in Raleigh when a thunderstorm cut the power to the stage in the middle of "Promised Land," forcing the band to retreat and then return a few minutes later to pick up the song exactly where they had left off. (Come to think of it, Bruce Hornsby was on stage for that show, too.)

Tuesday's second set started out strongly with good versions of "Victim," "Eyes," "Looks Like Rain" and "Terrapin." After drums/space we got the second half of "Playin," which the band started Sunday at Buckeye Lake. The second set pooped out for me after that, but I've lost my enthusiasm for "Wheel," "Throwing Stones > Not Fade Away" and "U.S. Blues" for the encore. The songs were well played, though.

All in all, a good run. The boys are on a roll and Tourheads who began in Deer Creek (an amphitheater outside of Indianapolis) say they've improved with every show.

So what will we hear tonight? My money's on "Help > Slip > Franklin's Tower" to open the second set, with either "Deal" or "Might As Well" to close the first set. "Bertha," "Greatest Story," "Black Peter," "Tennessee Jed," "Good Lovin'" and "Mighty Quinn" still haven't been played on this leg of the tour. (Most of those tunes were played in LA, though.)

News...News...News...

Die Scalper Scum! Tickets were a breeze in Charlotte. Could hardly give 'em away!...The cool sticker award for so far this summer goes to the sticker seen at the L.A. Shows "I'm tripping, and I can't get down!"...East Coast Fall Tour plans for the boys look like Philly Spectrum, Boston Garden and Madison Square Garden for 6, 9 & 6 nights respectively in September. This is strictly tentative so please do not call the venues or the Grateful Dead office for information regarding these shows until they are announced on the hotline. (East) 201-488-9393 (West) 415-457-6388. For more information regarding the Grateful Dead, subscribe to Unbroken Chain for $10/yr (6 issues). Make checks payable to Unbroken Chain, P.O. Box 8726, Richmond, VA 23226, or send a S.A.S.E. (#10) and $1.00 for a sample issue.

3/20
-Set I-
Hell In A Bucket
Althea
That Same Thing
Brown-Eyed Women
Mexicali Blues →
Maggie's Farm
Birdsong →
Promised Land

-Set II-
Shakedown Street
Women Are Smarter →
Dark Star →
Drums →
The Other One →
Standing On The Moon →
Turn On Your Lovelight
-ENCORE-
U.S. Blues

GATES OPEN 6:30PM
GRATEFUL DEAD
$22.50 U.S.
COPPS COLISEUM
GST INCLUDED
SAT MAR 21/92 7:30P
MADULT $26.50
SEC   ROW   SEAT
113R   19   9
AISLE 30

GRATEFUL DEAD
20 March 1992
Sometimes We Live
No Particular Way
But Our Own
Copps Coliseum
ccc

Wake up to find out that
you are the Eyes of the World

3/21
-Set I-
Help On The Way
Slipknot
Franklin's Tower
Little Red Rooster
Pretty Peggy O'
Queen Jane Approximately
✶ So Many Roads

-Set II-
✶✶ Long Way To Go Home →
✶✶✶ Corinna →
Terrapin Station →
Drums →
Last Time →
Black Peter →
One More Saturday Nite
-ENCORE-
Box of Rain

Apollo 11 25

Air Garcia

GRATEFUL DEAD
21 March 1992
Sometimes We Visit
Your Country And Live
In Your Home
Hamilton, Ontario
ccc

we're on County Highway C or some such dinky little country road on the way into Alpine Valley. We come around a bend and Burns takes a big swig of his beer. Out of nowhere there are flashing lights and a cop coming up fast. I figure it can't be the beer because this is Wisconsin, for God's sakes, where they make all the beer, right? But he signals for us to pull over, and ~~as soon~~ I do as soon as I see a shoulder wide enough for a car. The cop, a young dude, takes his time running my NJ plates before he comes up to the car and asks for my paperwork. Then he gives me, Burns, and the back seat the once over, looking for a probable cause, I'm sure, to tear the car apart. Finally, he says, "Drinking and driving is illegal in this state."

BAD COP, NO DONUT.

As politely as I can, I say, "I wasn't drinking, officer."
"Driving with a passenger who's drinking is illegal. Please follow me — if you do not, resisting arrest will be added to the charges." So we follow him to a clearing about a mile away, where they've got 2 tents set up and a bunch of bummed 'Heads are standing around. The cop who processes me tells me I've got an $82 fine. I tell him I don't have that much on me.
"You can pay with a credit card. If you can't pay, you'll face incarceration."
Burns says to me, "Go for that, Man!"
The cop looks at Burns, annoyed, and says, "Incarceration means prison."
I pull out all I've got and get the rest from Burns. It's all over in 15 minutes and we don't miss a lick of the show. I have to give up touring with Burns — he's dumb and dangerous.

In the attics of my life   Full of cloudy dreams unreal
Full of tastes no tongue can know   And lights no eye can see
When there was no ear to hear   You sang to me.

where all the pages are my days   And all my lights grow old
When I had no wings to fly   You flew to me.

I have spent my life   Seeking all that's still unsung   Bent my ear to hear the tune
And closed my eyes to see   When there were no strings to play   You played to me.

In the secret space of dreams   Where I dreaming lay amazed
When the secrets all are told   And the petals still unfold
When there was no dream of mine   You dreamed of me.

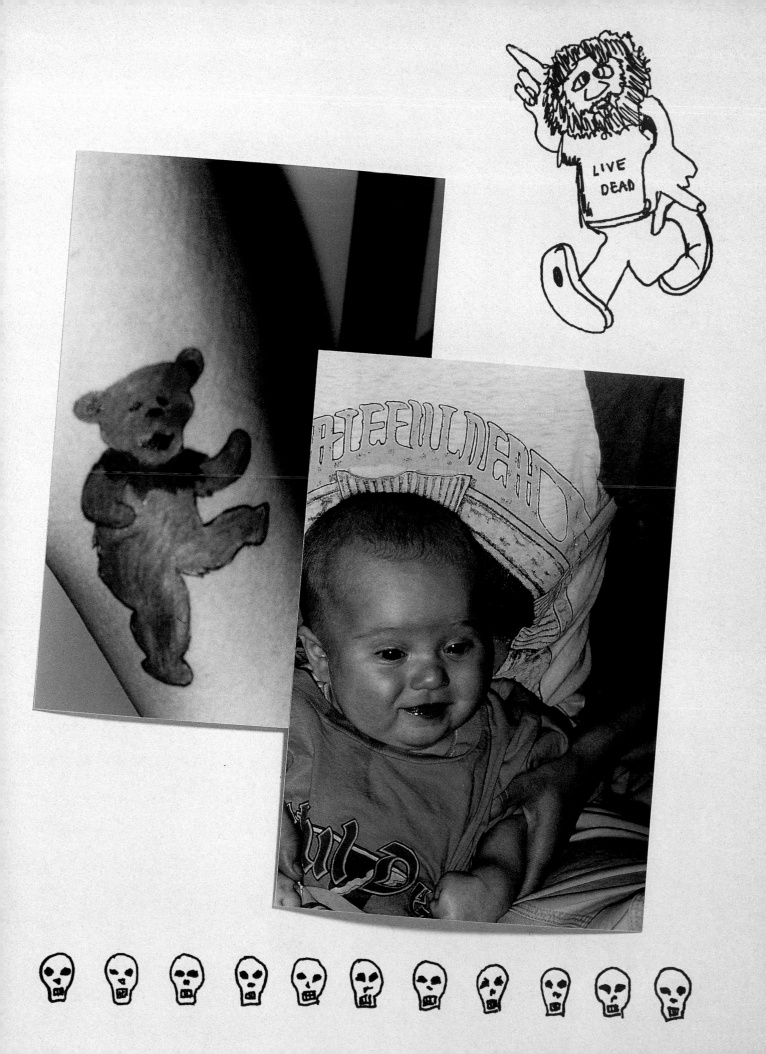

Tuner, Maximum Mike
and What's Her Name

HAPPY CAMPERS

<u>Camping 101:</u>
It's best to avoid pitchin' your tent after dark with a buzz on.

There could be rocks or even concrete where you put those stakes.

Other campers may even laugh at you.

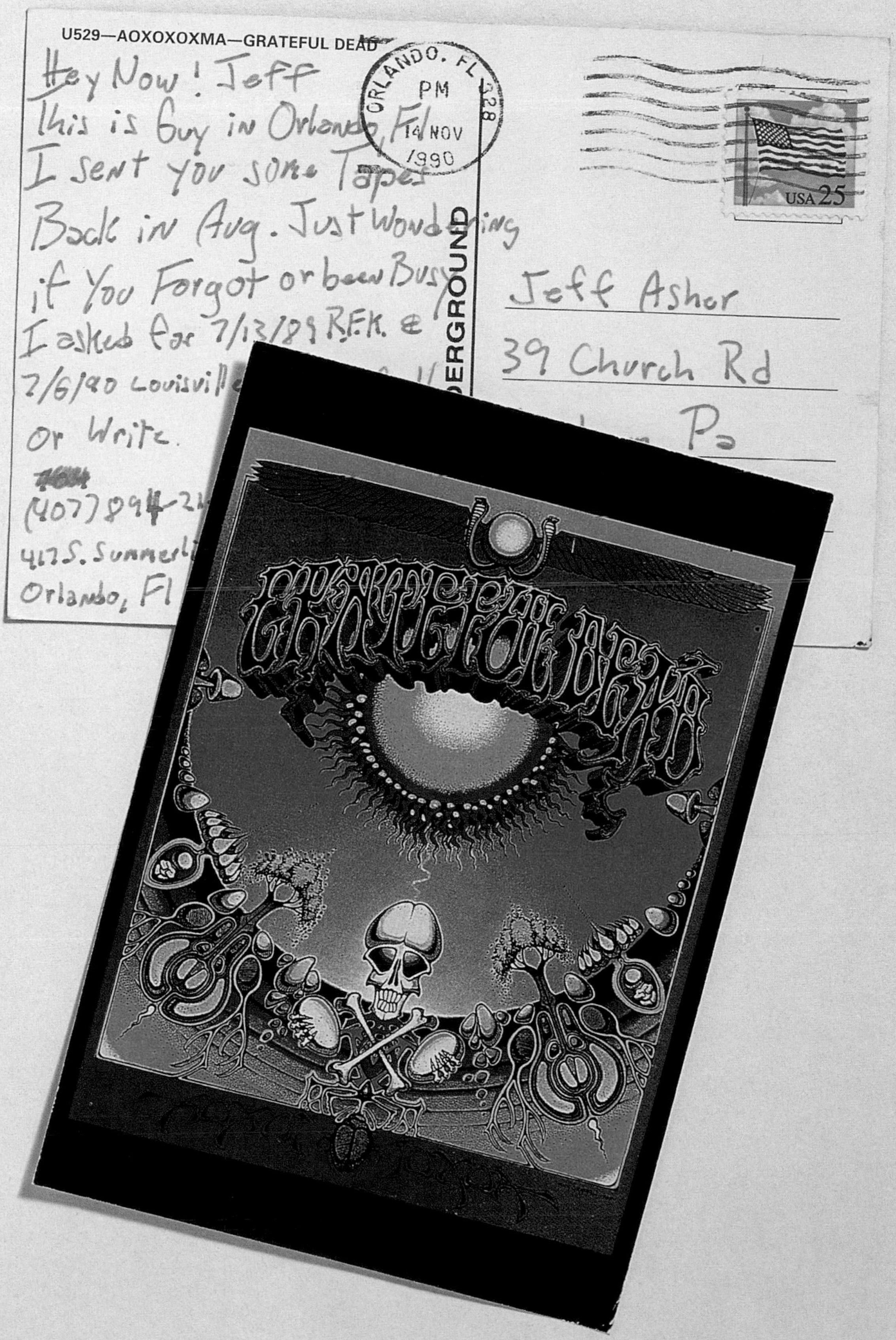

Hey Now! Jeff
This is Guy in Orlando, Fl
I sent you some Tapes
Back in Aug. Just Wondering
if You Forgot or been Busy
I asked for 7/13/89 R.F.K. &
2/6/90 Louisville
or Write.

(407) 894-2...
417 S. Summerl...
Orlando, Fl

UNDERGROUND

ORLANDO, FL 228
PM
14 NOV
1990

USA 25

Jeff Asher
39 Church Rd
... Pa

She's got everything delightful, she's got everything I need...

It's one in 10,000 that comes for the show...

↑Don't go straight!
Ripplewood bar. still water.

Heff →

to night... smell... redwood
when she is just...
Go Ask Alice...
PHILOSOPHIZED
OFF AT THE BEACH AND
AND MOLERA St. Park. off of
Canyon

I smell Brownies

STAYED IN PETALUMA

1/2/92
DROVE TO SCOTT I
MEAN ERICS IN SAN ANSELMO
GOT CAMPING EQUIPMENT
AND HEADED DOWN COAST
WATCHED SUNSET N. OF
BIG SUR WOW
1/3/92
ⓒ WOKE UP AT PFEIFFER
BIG SUR STATE PARK (DON'T
KNOW HOW) GOT B-FAST AND
A CABIN   WENT TO   over

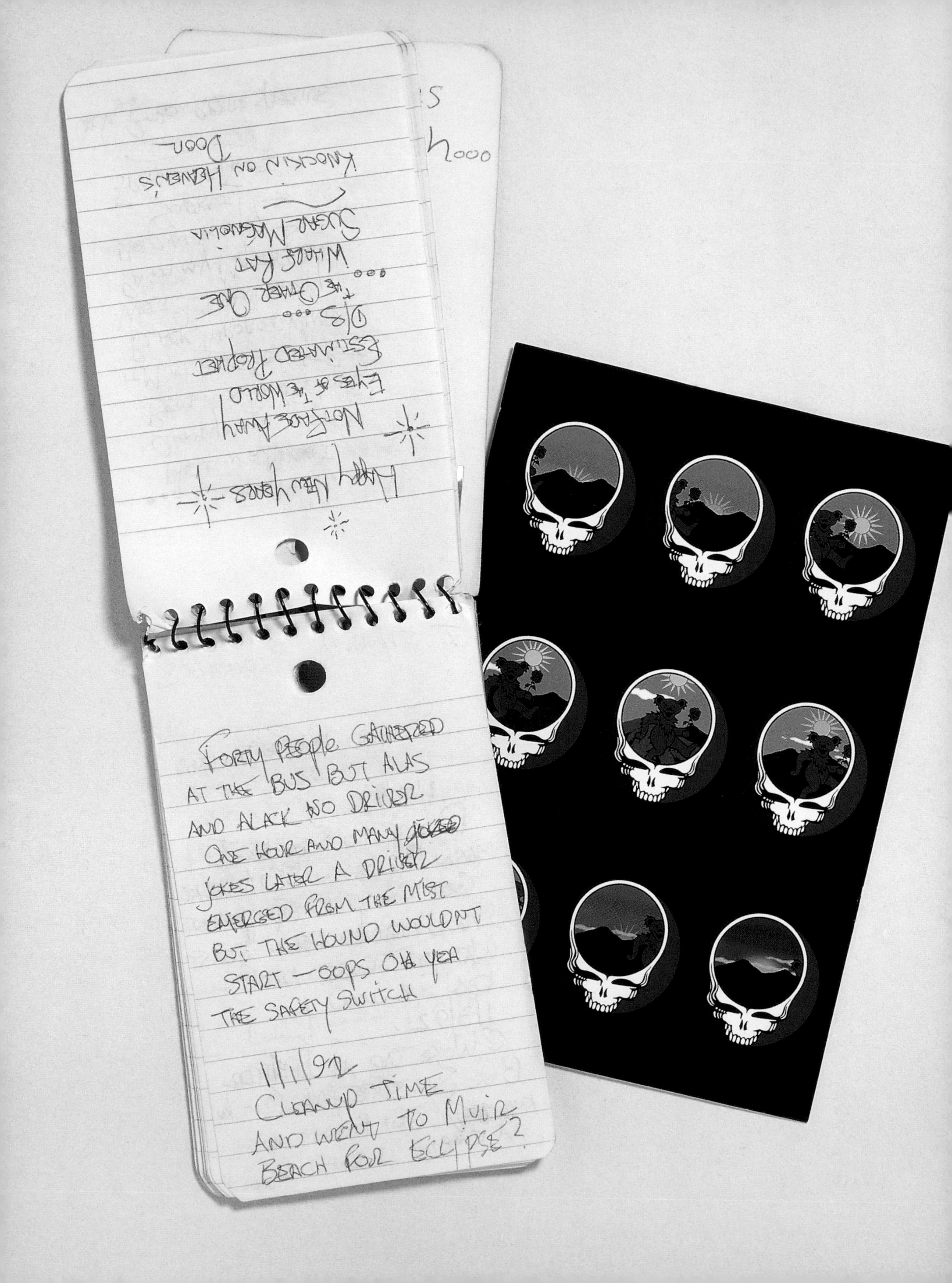

knockin on Heaven's
Door
Sugar Magnolia
Whale Rat
... the Other One
D/S ...
Estimated Prophet
Eyes of the World
Not Fade Away
Happy New Years
4000

Forty people gathered
at the bus but alas
and alack no driver
One hour and many jokes
jokes later a driver
emerged from the mist
but the hound wouldn't
start —oops oh yea
the safety switch

11/1/92
Cleanup time
and went to Muir
beach for eclipse?

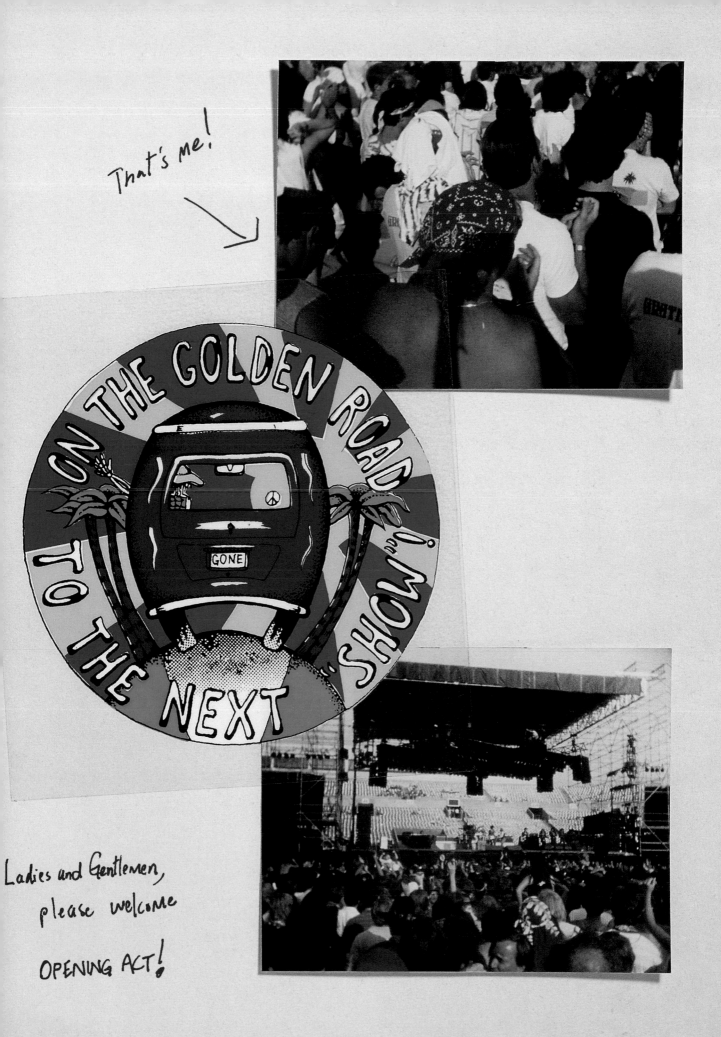

That's me!

ON THE GOLDEN ROAD TO THE NEXT SHOW!

GONE

Ladies and Gentlemen, please welcome

OPENING ACT!

CHINESE LUNAR YEAR 4691 ✤ YEAR OF THE ROOSTER
GUNG HAY FAT CHOY/MAY THE NEW YEAR BRING YOU HEALTH, HAPPINESS, AND PROSPERITY

The Chinese celebrate both the opening and the closing of the year. The closing, or end of a year is observed in a quiet way; a time for family to gather and reflect upon the positive and negative aspects of the previous year, recall communal gains and losses, and assess together the possibilities of renewal, faith, and hope. Individual family members allow each other the opportunity to resolve feuds and difficulties prior to the larger gathering, enabling themselves the ability to begin the new year in balance and harmony. The opening, or beginning of the year occurs nearly a week later, and is a time of boisterous and spectacular celebration. Traditionally, it is believed essential to recognize the presence of intense energy, both joyous and calamitous, that accompanies the opening of the year, and to consciously and respectfully direct the positive, and vigorously repel the negative.

SYMBOLS, ARCHTYPES, AND DEITIES

THE DRAGON A composite creature; with the head of a camel, horns of a deer, eyes of a rabbit, ears of a cow, neck of a snake, belly of a frog, scales of a carp, claws of a hawk, and the palms of a tiger, the Dragon is a symbol of the Emperor, representing the yang principle. His appearance at the new year brings the energy of Heaven down to the Earth.

THE PHOENIX This scarlet bird is the symbol of the Empress, and represents the yin principle. Her appearance in tandem with the Dragon signifies the balance between Heaven and Earth.

THE PEARL Appearing from amongst the clouds, the Pearl of Wisdom entices the Dragon, who brings the celestial energy to Earth in his pursuit of the jewel.

THE LIONS Emblems of strength and heralds of auspicious events, Lions are representative of the discipline and focus of the martial arts, and are seen throughout the year.

THE ROOSTER The opening of Chinese lunar year 4691 brings the Rooster, a creature who symbolizes the warmth and light of the universe. This particular Rooster has water as its element, and is influenced by the yin principle. The Water Rooster is intellectual, with tremendous energy and initiative. The Water Rooster is clear-headed and practical, and will not be prone to the strut and drone of some of the other roosters.

THE FLAGS The symbols represented on the flags in this pageant are known as the Eight Auspicious Symbols. They are: The Eternal Knot (Love); The Perfect Lotus; The Celestial Voice of Buddha (Conch); The Umbrella of Protection; The Two Fishes that Leap Free of the Water; The Banner to Proclaim the Water of Life; a ... aw/Vase of Jewels.

THE GODS OF WAR, PROSPERITY, AND LONGEVITY The ... respected deities. The God of War has as his chief attribute... example, the individuals' attainment of ultimate potential in... spiritual. He is the patron saint of small businesses and g... literature and scholarly pursuits. The God of Prosperity en... plenty, but especially the harmony inherent in having the ... potential. The God of Longevity is recognized by his dome... staff. Associated with the peach, a symbol of immortality, he is ... surrounded by mushrooms.

Please come look at our photo display in the lobby
showing the history of our dragon *Flash*

Urgent ☐

For _____

Date _____ Time _____

While You Were Out

M _____

Of _____

Phone _____

AREA CODE   NUMBER   EXTENSION

Telephoned ☐   Please Call ☐

Came To See You ☐   Will Call Again ☐

Returned Your Call ☐ Wants To See You ☐

Message

WERE AT THE BREW PUB. ASK FOR DIRECTIONS FB 2:26p.

Signed _____

9711   ☐ you!   ◆ ADAMS BUSINESS FORMS

ALES From THE LIGHTHOUSE BREW PUB

Lincoln City, Oregon

Speed and Trixie got a deal on a room at the Hyatt. Everybody is soaked with sweat after a hot day at R.F.K., so they invited 6 or 7 of their closest friends to use the shower. Mr. **E**nterprising **V**alet comes to the room with an offer to do the laundry. They hand over T-shirts, short whatever, and thank him a lot.

Mr. EV brought all the clothes back, T-shirts on hangers, smiling and thanking them. The crew dropped a sweet $50 on Mr. EV, thanking him for his kindness. Speed and Trixie felt a whole lot less kind the next day when they saw the $160 dry-cleaning charge on their bill. Still, their T-shirts and shorts hadn't been as clean since before the tour started.

16 songs

DOUBLETREE GUEST SUITES
TROY

I
Greatest Story
Bertha
Minglewood
Ramble On
Queen Jane
Lazy RvR. Road
Eternity
Don't Ease

II
Victim →
JAM ～
Foolish Heart
All too Much
Corrina
JAM
D/S
Last Time
S. O. T. M
Sugar Mags
(S.S.D.D.)
Liberty

Detroit 6/27/95

For Reservations Nationwide call 1-800-424-2900

Attack on Deadheads is no [?]

Band's followers handed stiff LSD sentences

By Dennis Cauchon
USA TODAY

David Chevrette was a young, free-spirited hippie.

His only possessions were his clothes, a dog and a 1970 Volkswagen bus painted with peace signs. For fun, he followed the Grateful Dead rock group on concert tours.

Then, the 20-year-old got busted for selling LSD in 1990 to a guy he met on the beach.

Now, he's doing 10 years without parole in federal prison — a longer sentence than those given in federal court to rapists, armed robbers and some big drug dealers.

Chevrette is a victim of a concerted crackdown on Grateful Dead fans — called Deadheads — and a quirk in federal drug law.

That quirk — involving whether to weigh the paper or sugar cube the LSD is stored on — has resulted in what Sen. Joseph Biden, D-Del., calls an "unintended inequity."

In short: LSD sentences are out of proportion — by a factor of 50 or more — with other drug sentences.

Chevrette's term for $1,500 worth of LSD is more severe than if he'd smuggled $100,000 worth of heroin.

The quirk — buried deep and unnoticed in a large drug law — has been turned into a bludgeon in the battle against Deadheads.

Today, 1,500 to 2,000 Deadheads are in prison, up from fewer than 100 four years ago. Most are young middle-class whites or old hippies. Many are serving mandatory no-parole prison terms of 10 or 20 years.

"We've opened a vein here," says Gene Haislip, head of LSD enforcement at the Drug Enforcement Administration. "We're going to mine it until this whole thing turns around."

The DEA has tripled spending, personnel and arrests for LSD since January 1990. "We've seen a marked pattern of LSD distribution at Grateful Dead concerts," says Haislip. "That has something to do with why so many (Deadheads) are arrested."

The Grateful Dead — top-grossing concert act last year ($34 million) — has been around since the 1960s.

Some people are weekend fans, such as Vice President-elect Gore

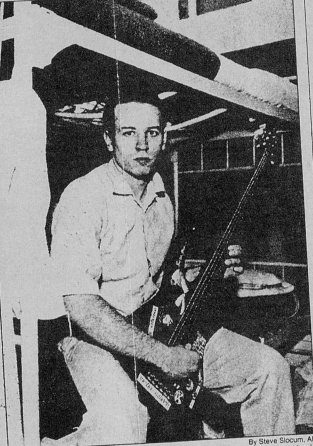

By Steve Slocum, AP

DOING TIME: Michael Thrasher, 19, in Sheridan, Ore., prison, where he is serving 10 years for possession of $2,000 worth of LSD — his first offense.

and his wife, Tipper, who took their daughter to a June Dead show.

Others are more devoted. They wear tie-dyed shirts and catch five or 10 shows a year.

The most dedicated fans follow the band from show to show, creating a traveling village of 3,000 to 6,000 sometimes called "Deadland."

The values are pure '60s: peace, love, vegetarianism, communal living and partying. To many, mind expansion is also part of the Deadhead experience — and that means LSD.

"Yes, LSD is my sacrament," says Franklin Martz, a Haight-Ashbury-born hippie who saw his first Grateful Dead show in 1967. He's now serving a 40-year LSD sentence.

This brazen advocacy of LSD angers many parents and police.

A USA TODAY review of more than 30 Deadhead cases found they routinely have their musical tastes, dress and lifestyle used against them in the criminal justice system:

▶ **More police searches.** A University of New Hampshire police officer acknowledged to the student newspaper that he pulled over cars with Grateful Dead bumper stickers.

▶ **Bond denial.** Deadhead Janet Godwin's license plate was presented at her North Carolina bond hearing to prove she was a flight risk. The plate read RAMBROSE, after the Grateful Dead song Ramble on Rose.

▶ **Negative portrayal to jury and**

Quirk in law [?] heavily on se[?]

People imprisoned on fede[?] treated more harshly than oth[?] cause of a quirk in the law.

The 1986 law sets sentences [?] charges of possession, sale or c[?] like other drugs such as coca[?] by weight. It's sold by the dos[?]

A dose of pure LSD is so tin[?] sell. A penny weighs the same [?] make LSD usable, producers [?] thing big enough to sell.

An LSD crystal is droppe[?] and the solution is sprayed [?] paper or gel. The carrier cou[?] sugar cube or a glass of juice [?] no relation to the drug's pote[?]

Should the carrier be wei[?]

The issue wasn't discussed [?] There's no indication anyon[?]

The Justice Department c[?] law's wording to weigh only [?] ties would be comparable w[?]

But the Reagan Justice D[?] er's weight should be count[?] Court agreed, saying it was [?] make inequitable sentence[?]

Result: LSD sentences ar[?] not drug weight. Sentence [?]
▶ pure LSD, 10 months.
▶ on paper, five years.
▶ on sugar cubes, 16 yea[?]

When Sen. Joesph Bide[?] the Judiciary Committee, [?] put a correction in the 198[?] passed the Senate, but the [?] ing has happened in Cong[?]

news media. Police told th[?] that Michael Thrasher's 1,9[?] of LSD had a satanic symb[?] upside down pentagram. No [?] was made of the word [?] stamped across the LSD pa[?]

The jury learned that T[?] 19, a college student from [?] Ore., was in a band named [?] Jake's Psychedelic Jug Ba[?] boree and Wino Wrestling [?] big issue at my trial was m[?] tive lifestyle,'" Thrasher s[?]

▶ **Sentencing prejudic[?]** head Todd Davidson, 20, [?] to 20 years without parol[?] scribed in his pre-sentence [?] Florida as a member of th[?] follows the Grateful Dead [?]

▶ **Prison labels.** Richa[?] classified as "gang-affilia[?] Colorado prison system b[?] a Deadhead. That label — [?]

Copyright USA Today December 17, 1992

Repri[?]

lucination

The ABCs of LSD effects

LSD became popular in the 1960s and is used by an estimated 2.8 million people annually.

A Primer of Drug Action, a classic college psychopharmacology textbook, says of LSD:

▶ Its main effect is perceptual: sounds and sights become more vivid. Laughter and sorrow are easily evoked, sometimes simultaneously.

▶ Psychotic episodes that would normally have been suppressed sometimes occur.

▶ The drug loses half its potency in three hours, but effects last 10 to 12.

▶ Occasional use of LSD for experimental purposes does not induce physical damage.

▶ No overdoses have been reported, but flashbacks, accidents and suicides have.

---

for Crips, Bloods and mem- of Aryan Nation — is used to de- ne where a prisoner is placed er to curb gang violence. But a pacifist, complains: "I'm ex- to harsher conditions all be- I'm a Deadhead."

dine Strossen of the American Liberties Union says: "People dn't be singled out because lifestyles or musical tastes are opular with the majority." eadheads get few breaks behind scenes, too.

orth Carolina lawyer Charles wer entered into what he thought e routine plea talks for a client. was surprised to find prosecutors willing to deal. "They were power- y impacted by the fact that she s a Deadhead," he says.

Deadheads often are subject to at's known as "jurisdiction shop-

ping" — prosecuting a case where it gets the greatest punishment.

Thrasher was arrested and prosecuted entirely by local authorities.

But the case was switched from state to federal court to get a longer sentence. In state court, he would have gotten 16 months; in federal court, he got 10 years without parole.

Davidson, now 22, is scheduled to be released from prison on March 19, 2010. He'll be 40.

"I'd go back on tour in a heartbeat," Davidson says. "It was a big happy family." At least until the real world intruded.

"It's funny," says Deadhead Christopher Jones, who just finished an LSD sentence in Virginia. "Everyone is like 'We gotta be careful,' but everyone is doing the same old thing. You've still got idiots walking around shows yelling, 'Doses! Doses!'"

permission.

GRATEFUL DEAD

BOSTON GARDEN   BOSTON, MASSACHUSETTS
SERIES 1: SEPTEMBER 25, 26 & 27
SERIES 2: SEPT 29-30 & OCT 1   ALL SHOWTIMES: 7:30 PM

DEADHEAD INFORMATION

PLEASE SEE OTHER SIDE OF FLYER FOR MASS TRANSIT AND PARKING INFO

CALL WBCN'S CONCERT HOTLINE AT 617 536-7105 FOR SHOWDAY UPDATES

CAMPING: (PLEASE NOTE: NO CAMPING IS ALLOWED AROUND BOSTON GARDEN OR IN BOSTON OR CAMBRIDGE PARKS!)

Gloucester	Annisquam Campground	508 283-2992
Bellingham	Circle CG Farm	508 966-1136
Plymouth	Indianhead Campground	508 888-3688
Wrentham	KOA Campground Boston Hub	508 384-8930
Littleton	Minuteman KOA Campground	508 772-0042
Norwell	Norwell Campsites	617 871-0527
Middleboro	Plymouth Rock KOA Campground	508 947-6435
Westford	Wyman's Beach	508 692-6287

HOTELS: (Call ahead and make reservations early, September is the busiest month of the year for hotels in New England)

Boston International-AYH Hostel	12 Hemenway St	617 536-9455
Howard Johnson	575 Commonwealth Ave	617 267-3100*
Howard Johnson	1271 Boylston St	617 267-8300*
Howard Johnson Hotel Cambridge	777 Memorial Dr	617 492-7777*
Lenox Hotel	710 Boylston St	617 536-5300*
Holiday Inn-Boston Government Center	5 Blossom & Cambridge Sts	617 742-7630*
Midtown Hotel	220 Huntington Ave	617 262-1000*
Tremont House	275 Tremont St	617 426-1400*
Comfort Inn-Dedham	235 Elm St	617 326-6700*
Days Inn-Braintree	190 Wood Rd	617 848-1260*
Days Inn-Lexington	440 Bedford St	617 861-0850*
Holiday Inn-Dedham	Jct Us 1 & SR 128, exit 15A	617 329-1000*
The Inn at Children's	342 Longwood Ave	617 731-4700*
Howard Johnson Lodge-Braintree	150 Granite St	617 848-8500*
Quality Inn-Waltham	455 Totten Pond Rd	617 890-3000*
Susse Chalet-Dorchester	900 Morrissey Blvd	617 287-9200*
Terrace Lodge	1650 Commonwealth Ave & Mt Hood Rd Brighton	617 566-6260*

*restaurant, coffee shop, dining room or cafeteria adjacent or opposite

CHAMBER OF COMMERCE: 617 227-4500
HOSPITAL: Boston City Hospital   818 Harrison Ave   617 534-4075
AAA (Emergency road service):   800 222-4357

TAPING SECTION:
There will be a taping section at all of these shows. This will be the only place that taping will be allowed. Tape anywhere else and you will be told to leave the concert. You must have a **reserved taper's ticket** in order to tape. One audio cassette deck per person. No reel-to-reel. Taping is for non-commercial, home use only. Unauthorized broadcast, duplication, distribution or sale is strictly forbidden!!!

ABSOLUTELY NO VIDEO EQUIPMENT OF ANY KIND!!!!!!!!!!

Photo © Joe Ryan

© W.J.D. 6/27/94 (w/special Shoreline assist by M.A.S.)

VERMONT 7/13

LIGTR
JACKSTRAW
ALTHEA
QUEEN JANE
LOSER
ALL OVER NOW
TEN JED
LET IT GROW

TRUCKIN
SPEEDWAY (SOTM)
WAY to Go
CORRINA
UNCLE JOHNS
DJS

GD 1/1/94 – 6/30/94 Analysis		
Song	Totals Shows	
1 Way to Go Home	12	
2 Lazy River Road	11	
3 I Fought the Law	9	
4 This Could Be the Last Time	9	
5 Corrina	8	
6 Don't Ease Me In	8	
7 Easy Answers	8	
8 El Paso	8	
9 I Need a Miracle	8	
10 Liberty	8	
11 Ramble On Rose	8	
12 Standing on the Moon	8	
13 Eyes of the World	7	
14 He's Gone	7	
15 Playin' in the Band	7	
16 Stella Blue	7	
17 Wang Dang Doodle	7	
18 When I Paint My Masterpiece	7	
19 All Along the Watchtower	6	
20 Estimated Prophet	6	
21 Eternity	6	
22 Ko Ko	6	
23 Jack Straw	6	
24 Loose Lucy	6	
25 Other One	6	
26 Peggy-O	6	
27 Saint of Circumstance	6	
28 Sugar Magnolia	6	
29 Terrapin Station	6	
30 Throwing Stones	6	
31 Uncle John's Band	6	
32 U.S. Blues	6	
33 Wheel	6	
34 Althea	5	
35 Bird...	5	
... Sunflower	5	
... Mountain	5	
... Rider	5	
... Rooster	5	
... Stopped	5	
... approximately	5	
... Jilah	5	
...	5	
...	5	
... Lovelight	5	
... me	5	
...	5	
... Wind	4	
...	4	
...	4	
...	4	
...	4	
...	4	
...	4	
...	4	
...	4	
...	4	
...	4	
...	4	
...	4	
...	3	
...	3	
... Shakedown Palace	3	
84 Candyman	3	
85 Franklin's Tower	3	
86 Good Lovin'	3	
87 Greatest Story Ever Told	3	
88 Help on the Way	3	
89 If the Shoe Fits	3	
90 Johnny B. Goode	3	
91 Little Red Rooster	3	
92 Loser	3	
93 Man Smart Woman Smarter	3	
94 Shakedown Street	3	
95 Slipknot	3	
96 Stagger Lee	3	
97 That Would Be Something	3	
98 West L.A. Fadeaway	3	
99 Beat It On Down the Line	2	
100 Black Peter	2	
101 Cold Rain & Snow	2	
102 Cumberland Blues	2	
103 Dark Star	2	
104 Goin' Down The Road Feeling Bad	2	
105 Let it Grow	2	
106 Let the Good Times Roll	2	
107 Maggie's Farm	2	
108 Mama Tried	2	
109 Mexicali Blues	2	
110 New Speedway Boogie	2	
111 Spoonful	2	
112 Sugaree	2	
113 Beer Barrel Polka	1	14–Jun
114 Big Railroad Blues	1	08–Jun
115 Desolation Row	1	31–Mar
116 Dire Wolf	1	01–Apr
117 High Time	1	16–Mar
118 It Must've Been the Roses	1	28–Mar
119 King Bee	1	31–Mar
120 Knockin' On Heaven's Door	1	19–Jun
121 Might as Well	1	23–Mar
122 Ship of Fools	1	05–Jun
123 Sunshine Daydream (separate)	1	10–Jun
124 Turn on Your Lovelight (reprise)	1	05–Jun
125 Weight, The	1	25–Mar
Total songs, 1/1/94 – 6/30/94	543	
Total shows, 1/1/94 – 6/30/94	34	
Songs / show, 1/1/94 – 6/30/94	15.971	
1st set songs, 1/1/94 – 6/30/94	252	7.412
2nd set songs, 1/1/94 – 6/30/94	257	7.559
Encores, 1/1/94 – 6/30/94	34	1.000

GRATEFUL DEAD
PLUS SPECIAL GUEST: STING
GIANTS STADIUM   EAST RUTHERFORD, NEW JERSEY
JUNE 5 & 6, 1993   BOTH SHOWTIMES: 6 PM
DEADHEAD INFORMATION

NOTE: THERE WILL BE NO VENDING, CAMPING OR OVERNIGHT PARKING ALLOWED OUTSIDE OR INSIDE ANY OF THE FACILITIES ON THE 1993 SUMMER TOUR.

DOORS TO THE STADIUM WILL OPEN AT 4 PM ON BOTH SHOWDAYS AND THE PARKING LOTS WILL BE OPEN AT 1 PM. PLEASE DO NOT ARRIVE EARLY.

CAMPING:

Clinton	Round Valley State Park	908 236-6355
Clinton	Spruce Run Recreation Area	908 638-8572
Clinton	Voorhees State Park	908 638-6969
Hackettstown	Allamuchy State Park	908 852-3790
Hope	Jenny Jump State Forest	908 459-4366
Matawan	Cheesequake State Park	908 566-2161
Netcong	Fla-Net Park	908 347-4467

HOTELS:

Quality Inn	10 Polito Ave	Lyndhurst	201 933-9800*
Days Inn-Meadowlands	850 SR 120	East Rutherford	201 507-5222*
Sheraton Meadowlands	2 Meadowlands Plaza	East Rutherford	201 896-0500*
Turnpike Motel	Route 46	West Ridgefield	201 943-2500
Plaza Motor Inn	155 Route 3	East Secaucus	201 348-8300*
Days Hotel	455 Harmon Meadow Blvd	Secaucus	201 617-8888*
Holiday Inn Sportsplex	300 Plaza Dr	Secaucus	201 348-2000*
Ramada Plaza	350 Route 3 West Mill Creek Dr	Secaucus	201 863-8700*
Meadowlands Hilton	2 Harmon Plaza	Secaucus	201 348-6900*
Red Roof Inn	15 Meadowlands Pkwy	Secaucus	201 319-1000
Inn at Ramsey	1315 Route 17 S	Ramsey	201 327-6700*
Howard Johnson Motor Lodge	1255 Route 17 S	201 327-4500*	
Wellesley Inn by Howard Johnson	946 Route 17 N	Ramsey	201 934-9250*
Holiday Inn	50 Route 17 N	Paramus	201 843-5400*
Howard Johnson Lodge	393 State Route 17	Paramus	201 265-4200*
Radisson Paramus	601 Fromm Rd	Paramus	201 262-6900*

*restaurant, dining room, cafeteria or coffee shop adjacent or opposite

CHAMBER OF COMMERCE: (Meadowlands)   201 939-0707
HOSPITAL: Meadowlands Hospital   Meadowlands Pkwy Secaucus   201 392-3100
AAA (Emergency road service):   201 435-2121 or 201 265-2121
24 HOUR GAS: Stations along Routes 17 & 3

TAPING SECTION:
There will be a reserved taper's section at these shows, in the stands behind the lighting platform. This is the only place that taping will be allowed so do not tape anywhere else or you will be told to leave the concert. You must have a **marked reserved taper's ticket** in order to tape. Please note that taper's **will not** be let in early for these shows as their seats are reserved and in the stands. One audio cassette tape deck per person. No reel-to-reel. Taping is for non-commercial, home use only! Unauthorized broadcast, duplication, distribution or sale is strictly forbidden!!!!!!!

ABSOLUTELY NO VIDEO EQUIPMENT OF ANY KIND!!!!!!

BOOK PARTY? DO BOOKS BURN?

GRATEFUL DEAD TICKET SALES
MAIL ORDER INSTRUCTIONS
REVISED JANUARY 29, 1995

PLEASE SEND YOUR FUTURE ORDERS IN A #10 SIZED ENVELOPE. MAKE SURE THAT YOUR
RETURN NAME, ADDRESS, THE CONCERT DATES AND HOW MANY TICKETS TO EACH CONCERT
YOU WANT ARE ON THE OUTSIDE OF YOUR ORDER TO US! INCLUDE THE FOLLOWING:

1)   A 3X5 index card
files and may get lost.
your full name, address a
important in case your ti
is some other problem).
preference. "Anything Ava
insure that you get somet
offering both reserved an
insure that you have the
"anything" means that if
any tickets. For multipl
that you'll accept any ti

2)   Include a POSTAL
ORDER made payable to: GR
exact amount necessary.
Make sure your name and a
If your order is not fill
PERSONAL CHECKS AND NO C

3)   Also include a #
tickets. PLEASE do not de
mention of tickets. It
with care!) We do love a
envelopes.

4)   One order per en
fill out his or her own
disqualification of all i

5)   If we announce m
maximum number of tickets
state otherwise. Mixed
one envelope will not be

6)   All orders will
postmark, NOT by when we
Metered mail includes pos
FEDERAL EXPRESS ACCEPTED!
will announce it on the
postmarked the first day
automatically becomes a

7)   You may have you
$6.75 to your money order
for registration. Rememb
forget to put regular pos

8)   The hotlines lis
info. Follow all hotline
differs from the above,

Grateful Dead Ticket Sales
Returned Order Notice
Revised January 29, 1995

We are sorry to inform you that we could not fill your request because:

1)   POSTAL OR AMERICAN EXPRESS MONEY ORDERS ONLY!! NO CASH/
        PERSONAL CHECKS.
2)   NO SELF-METERED MAIL.
3)   NO SELF-ADDRESSED, STAMPED ENVELOPE ENCLOSED*
4)   WRONG SIZE ENVELOPE - *BOTH* ENVELOPES MUST BE A #10 SIZE*
5)   NO 3X5 INDEX CARD OR WRONG SIZE(PAPER DOES NOT COUNT AS CARD)
6)   INCOMPLETE INFORMATION ON INDEX CARD:

        A)   NO NAME AND/OR ADDRESS
        B)   NO DATE PREFERENCE LISTED
        C)   NO PRICE PREFERENCE LISTED

7)   YOUR REQUEST WAS MAILED TO THE WRONG ADDRESS*
8)   YOUR REQUEST WAS POSTMARKED TOO EARLY/TOO LATE*
9)   NO RETURN ADDRESS ON THE OUTSIDE OF THE ORDER TO US*
(10)   WRONG $ WAS __146⁵⁰_____   SHOULD BE __146 75_____
11)   ORDERED MORE THAN THE _____ MAXIMUM PER CONCERT*
12)   NO CONCERT NAME, DATE OR SERIES ON THE OUTSIDE OF ORDER TO US
13)   NO MIXED CITY OR SERIES ORDERS ACCEPTED

14)   OTHER_____
15)   WE WERE SOLD OUT BY THE TIME WE GOT TO YOUR ORDER

HOTLINES:

        CALIFORNIA HOTLINE: 415 457-6388
        EAST COAST HOTLINE: 201 744-7700
        TICKET PROBLEMS: 415 457-8034 (11 AM - 5 PM CALIF.
                                             TIME MONDAY-FRIDAY)
        GD MERCHANDISING: 800 225-3323 (NO TICKET INFO EVER!)

SUGGESTIONS, COMMENTS, COMPLAINTS, PRAISE, ETC.   WRITE TO US AT:
                        GDTS-COMMENTS
                         PO BOX 9812
                  SAN RAFAEL, CALIFORNIA 94912

        NEVER SEND ORDERS TO THIS ADDRESS. THEY WON'T BE FILLED!!!!

*SO MANY PEOPLE FILLED OUT THEIR REQUESTS CORRECTLY THAT IT WOULD HAVE BEEN
UNFAIR TO THEM TO FILL YOUR REQUEST FIRST. WHEN WE GET AN INCORRECT REQUEST,
WE PUT IT ASIDE UNTIL ALL CORRECT ORDERS ARE FILLED. THEN WE FILL THE
"PROBLEM" REQUESTS IF THERE ARE ANY TICKETS LEFT. WE ARE TRYING TO BE AS FAIR
AS POSSIBLE TO EVERYONE, BUT AS USUAL THERE WILL BE SOME PEOPLE LEFT UNHAPPY.
WE ARE SORRY ABOUT THIS AND APPRECIATE YOUR BUSINESS.

                ALWAYS LISTEN TO THE HOTLINE FOR CORRECT INFORMATION
                        THANK YOU AND STAY IN TOUCH
                        THE DEAD DUCATS CREW

Should have learned to add!

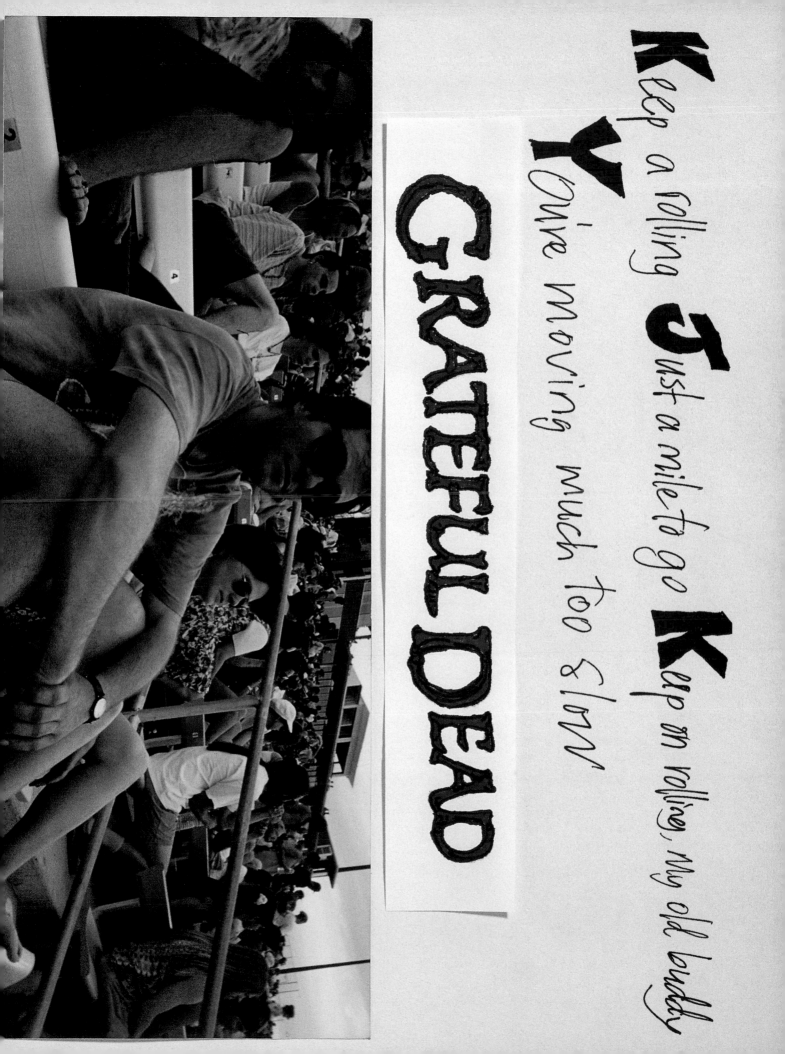

Keep a rolling **J**ust a mile to go
Keep on rolling, my old buddy
You're moving much too slow

GRATEFUL DEAD

This fractal image was generated using an IBM 3090-600E supercomputer at the Cornell Nation[al] Supercomputer Facility, a resource of the Corn[ell] Theory Center. Fractals, which are a result [of] repetitive mathematical computation, are used [to] model phenomena in fields ranging from a[s]tronomy to zoology.

PLEASE WRITE YOUR NAME AND ADDRESS BELOW AND RETURN THIS CARD TO US SO THAT WE MIGHT HAVE YOUR ADDRESS ON OUR MAILING LIST.

ART MATRIX
P. O. BOX 880
ITHACA, N. Y. 14851
U.S.A.
TEL: (607) 277-0959
Return Postage Guaranteed

From even deeper in The Vault...Dick's Picks Vol. Two! For those who have been clamoring for a worthy successor to the wildly successful One and Two From The Vault, comes something a little different. Dick's Pick's is a series of live releases carefully selected by the Grateful Dead's intrepid vault custodian, Dick Latvala, and lovingly edited and mastered by the Dead's team of audio alchemists. This is the real, raw stuff. Direct from the original two-track tapes, with no chance to "fix the mix". Unlike the "From The Vault" series, we didn't have access to complete shows. The source tapes had good old-fashioned glitches, splices and gaps due to reel changes. Some editorial surgery was required. We feel the historical value and musical quality of these tapes more than compensate for any sonic anomalies.

The first "Dick's Picks" is from the Dead's final show of 1973, on December 19th at Curtis Hixon Convention Center in Tampa, FL. This is a period that Latvala describes as "just chock full of killer shows". "Dick's Pick Vol. 2" is from Columbus Ohio Halloween 1971, and is just as captivating. The CD holds an hour long jam including Dark Star, Sugar Magnolia, St. Stephen, Not Fade Away, Going Down The Road, back into Not Fade...whew! Dick's Pick Vol. 2 is a must-have for every serious Deadhead and is available now by mail order only.
To order call 1-800-323-2300 or send $13.50 to Dick's Picks Vol. Two Box 2139 Dept. 2 Novato CA 94948 California residents add 7.25% sales tax.

DICK'S PICKS

GRATEFULDEAD

Tuna in Tempe

Casual guy

Put that in your ear
and smoke it.

Shooter Joe is a student photographer who loves the Dead. He sends a fax to Dennis McNally, the guy who deals with press for the band, and requests a photo pass for Giant's Stadium '95. McNally calls back 2 weeks later, telling Joe that he can take pictures for the 1st three songs from Phil's side of the stage on the 2nd night of the stand.

Shooter shot about 12 rolls of film during those 3 songs. At one point, Bobby starts making, like, these goofy rock 'n roll expressions for the camera, then he'd peek over at Jerry and they'd burst up laughing about it.
Jerry smiles for the camera, which Shooter says is like a lightning bolt from Zeus.

Nothin' left to do but smile, smile, smile

Dizzy With Eternity

GREENPEACE
YOU CAN'T SINK A RAINBOW

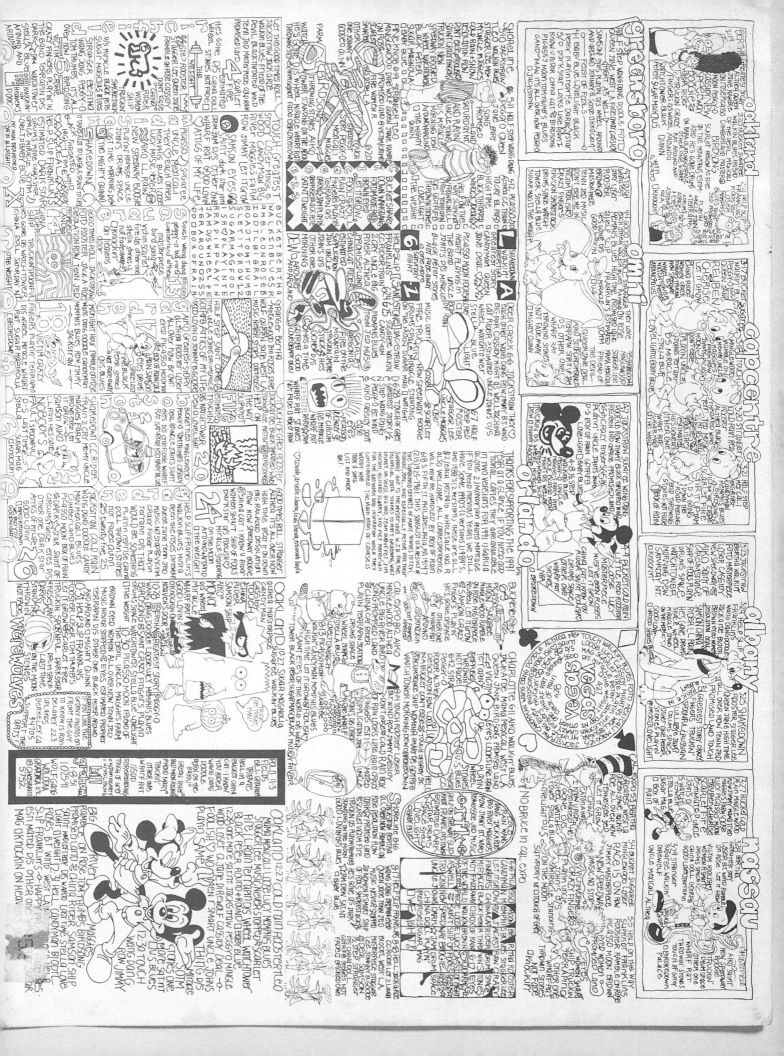

You ain't gonna learn
what you don't want to know.

But the heat came round and busted me for smilin' on a cloudy day.

The bus came along and I got on
That's when it all began.

WE CAN HAVE HIGH TIMES
IF YOU'LL
ABIDE.

Plungin' like stones from a slingshot from Mars.

standing on the moon, but I would rather be with you, I'd rather be with you

My last show

FEY CONCERTS PRESENTS
GRATEFUL DEAD
TUESDAY NOVEMBER 29, 199
MCNICHOLS ARENA
7:00 PM

GRATEFUL DEAD
DENVER, COLORADO
McNICHOLS SPORTS ARENA
NOT GOOD FOR ADMISSION
11 • 29 • 94
GUEST

IF YOU DO THIS FOR ME I'LL
GRANT YOU SEXUAL FAVORS.

630524 ©RPP, Inc. DALE

Backstage Pass — a can of Coke,
a free sandwich, a chance to watch
the crew hustle and bustle, a
glimpse of the band as they
head for the stage.

Blow here

DUPREE'S DIAMOND NEWS

Published by Sally Ansorge Mulvey, John Dwork,
Heidi Kelso, and Mark Frisk

No. 25D — Nassau, NY
March/April 1993 — Free Handout

DDN NOTES

• **LOST & FOUND** — Many of you probably read in our last tour-flyers that on March 11, after the show at the Rosemont Horizon in Illinois, a car was stolen, and in it was a brown backpack with original GD artwork, belt buckles, and photographs by/belonging to Owsley (Bear). The extended GD Family got together and did a major networking search via flyers and word-of-mouth, and IT WORKED!!! Apparently a young kid had brought the merchandise into a local Illinois store called "The Parking Lot, Inc." to sell and the rest is history. No police were involved and no arrest made. Bear just wanted his artwork back, and said, "I hope this kid learns a great life lesson." We do, too!

• The Dead cancelled their March 13, Ridgefield, OH, show due to snow — first time since '74. To make up the financial loss, they added two shows at the end of the tour at Nassau Coliseum. A lucky break for all those who got shut out for Albany/Nassau tix!

• It took only 20 minutes for the Sunday Nassau show to be sold out, and a lot longer — 2 hours — for the Monday night show. What's going on here?

• Long Island's only authorized Grateful Dead radio — Thursday nites, 10PM-Midnight — 88.5 WKWZ FM, *Remember Bill Graham*.

• **WBAI 99.5 FM Morning Dew** — Saturday nites 10PM-Midnight.

• **Amazon Week IV**, May 3-9 — call 212-219-2704 for more info.

• Jerry's health is much improved, he's lost about 60+ lbs, and he's working real hard to quit smoking. Rumor has it he's also very much in love. Don't be surprised to see him beaming onstage!

• There are five new songs so far: Liberty, a rewrite of the music of an old Hunter/Garcia tune; Lazy River Road, a Hunter/Garcia tune; Eternity, written by Bobby and Willie Dixon just prior to his death; Broken Arrow, a Robbie Robertson tune; and The Days Between, another Hunter/Garcia tune. They also broke out *I Fought The Law and The Law Won* — an interesting choice given the current climate! And *Lucy in the Sky with Diamonds* reappeared.

• At the February 23 Oakland show, Jerry's guitar fell and split at the pins just prior to show time. Did someone trip?

• Jerry is working on another album with David Grisman and the word is "don't be surprised if it's out before summer."

• Billy Kreutzmann, who likes to stay pretty much to himself, lately has been taking a strong stand with/for the homeless in California. He's also been getting involved on a greater level with the homeless problem in general.

• GD Merchandising is coming out with an exciting new product called: *Daily Tripper*, for all you Deadheads into computers, here's something you can't be without. It's a calendar/database filled with GD trivia. Retailing for $69.

• GDTS tells us that there were more ticket requests for this spring tour than *ever* before! They are also warning to beware of counterfeits in the parking lot!!!

• Getting hold of Dead tickets in New England, where the Dead haven't played in 18 months, was a horrendous mess! This spring, the closest the Dead got to New England was Albany. The Dead only received 7,000 tickets per show to distribute via mail order (the rest went to local ticketmaster offices). Unfortunately the Dead recieved 25,000 ticket orders per night for those same shows! The local concert promoter decided *not* to put tickets for these shows on sale via phone. As a result, one could only get tickets by standing in line in 10° snowy weather at local ticketmaster locations. In Pittsfield Massachussetts, 1300 people (many of whom drove hours to get to an Albany area ticketmaster) showed up for only 250 tickets and a near riot ensued with no line, no security and plenty of scalpers. This was very short-sighted

• **BUYER BEWARE.** there's a guy selling tickets through various ticket boards (one of them being 900-RUN-DEAD) who is selling hard-to-get tickets via the mail, but the tix never arrive, and the money's been sent. Be careful, many folks have been ripped off!

For subscription problems or change of address, call 914-232-6719 or write DDN, Box 148, Purdys, NY 10578

THIS IS A FREE HANDOUT. PLEASE DON'T LITTER!

ONE DOLLAR • DECEMBER 17, 1979

New West

Fifty Great
Books for Christmas

New Life
for the
Grateful Dead

By Charlie Haas

Road Crew

Last Stand for Our Western Forests

Special Pull-out Section:
California's French
Restaurants

Rosemont Horizon, Chicago, IL

March 9, 1993
Here Comes Sunshine
Wang Dang Doodle
Loose Lucy
Me & My Uncle>
Mexicali Blues
Broken Arrow
Row Jimmy
Eternity
Liberty

Chinc Cat Sunflower>
I Know You Rider
Victim or the Crime>
Ship of Fools
Playing in the Band>
Drums>Space>
The Last Time>
Black Peter>
Sugar Magnolia
*Knockin'
18 Songs

March 10, 1993
Feel Like A Stranger
Stagger Lee
The Same Thing
Peggy-O
Qn. Jane Appros.
Ramble On Rose
Let It Grow

Eyes of the World
Way To Go Home
Lazy River Road
Corinna>
Jam>Drums>Space>
The Wheel>
Watchtower>
Standing on the Moon>
NFA
*Baby Blue
16 Songs

March 11, 1993
Help On The Way>
Slipknot!>
Franklin's Tower*
Little Red Rooster
Althea
Masterpiece
So Many Roads
Music Never Stopped

Iko Iko
Wave to the Wind>
Truckin'>
Spoonful>
He's Gone>
Drums>Space^>
The Other One>
The Days Between>
Around 'n Around
*Liberty
17 Songs
^w/Ken Nordine

Ridgefield, OH

March 14, 1993
Cold Rain & Snow
Walkin'
Brown-Eyed Woman
Tom Thumb's Blues
Lazy River Road
Eternity
Don't Ease

Touch of Gray
Sampson & Delilah
Way To Go Home
Corinna>
Jam>Terrapin Station>
Drums>Space>
I Need A Miracle>
Stella Blue>
Throwin' Stones>
Lovelight
*I Fought The Law+
17 Songs
+ first time

Cap Center, Landover, MD

March 16, 1993
Jack Straw
Row Jimmy
New Minglewood Blues
So Many Roads
Cassidy
Tennessee Jed
Promised Land

Scarlet Begonias>
Fire on the Mtn
Women Are Smarter
Uncle John's Band>
Jam w/o Bob & Jerry>
Drums>Space>
The Last Time>
Morning Dew>
Sugar Magnolia
*US Blues
15 Songs

March 17, 1993
Shakedown Street
Wang Dang Doodle
Lazy River Road
Desolation Row
Ramble On Rose
Eternity
Liberty

Picasso Moon
Crazy Fingers>
Playing in the Band>
Dark Star (1st verse)>
Jam w/o Jerry
Drums>Space>Jam>
The Other One>
The Days Between>
Good Lovin'
*Lucy in the Sky
  w/Diamonds
15 Songs

March 18, 1993
Hell in a Bucket>
Sugaree
Walkin' Blues
Broken Arrow
Loose Lucy
Masterpiece
Friend of the Devil
Music Nvr Stopped

China Cat Sunflower>^
I Know You Rider^
Way to go Home
Wave to the Wind>^
Estimated Prophet>^
Terrapin Station>^
Drums>Space>^
Corrina>^
Wharf Rat>^
Throwin' Stones>^
NFA^
*I Fought The Law^
19 Songs

^w.Bruce Hornsby on Accordian

Dupree's Diamond News
The Ultimate Grateful Dead Fanzine

Four times per year our 64+ page version of DUPREE'S puts you right in the center of the Grateful Dead Experience with band interviews & news, in-depth concert & tape reviews, *every* set list, great GD photos & art, enlightening articles on environmental activism, Grateful Dead spirituality, fascinating interviews with the elders of our scene including: Ken Kesey, John Barlow, Tim Leary, Ram Dass, Terrence McKenna, and more!

HERE'S HOW TO SUBSCRIBE:

4 issues: US $14, Canada $18, Europe $26, Asia $30
(or $5.50 US for 1 sample copy).
4-issue subscription includes a 25-word tape ad (**no** personals), ad must accompany subscription request and will be published in first available issue of DDN. Please allow 6-8 weeks for delivery of first issue. Include: Name, Address, City/State, Zip, Phone #, and preference for current or next issue to start your subscription. Send check, money order, or cash (foreign subscribers money order or cash only) to: *(also makes a great gift)*

DUPREE'S DIAMOND NEWS
PO BOX 148, PURDYS, NY 10578

GD Hotline #s
East Coast 201-488-9393
West Coast 415-457-6388
Mail Order 415-457-8457
Problems 415-457-8034

BUILD YOUR OWN MUSICAL ADVENTURE

Highly skilled, versatile bass player/composer seeks gifted musicians for collaboration. My musical influences are World Beat, Funk, Psychedelic, & Jazz, and are strongly represented in my compositions. Strong desire and a sense of adventure are a must. If you seek creative fulfillment and have the will to go for it, call Michael at 914-232-6725.

Omni, Atlanta, GA

March 20, 1993
Mississippi Half-Step
It's All Over Now
So Many Roads
Me & My Uncle>
Maggie's Farm
Bird Song
Promised Land

Eyes of the World
Looks Like Rain
Lazy River Road
Truckin'>
Smokestack Lightenin'>
Drums>Space>
The Wheel>
Watchtower>
Standing on the Moon>
One More Saturday Nite
*Liberty
17 Songs

March 21, 1993
Feel Like A Stranger
West LA Fade Away
Black-Throated Wind
Candyman
Qn Jane Approx.>
Brown-Eyed Woman
Eternity
Liberty

Samson & Delilah
Way To Go Home
Broken Arrow
St. of Circumstance>
He's Gone>
Drums>Space>
I Need A Miracle>
The Days Between>
Around 'n Around
*Baba O'Riley
*Tomorrow Never Knows
18 Songs

March 22, 1993
Help On The Way>
Slipknot!>
Franklin's Tower>
Little Red Rooster
Althea
BIODTL>
Tom Thumb's Blues
Lazy River Road
Picasso Moon

Wave to the Wind
Iko Iko>
Corrina>
Uncle John's Band>
China Doll>
Drums>Space>
The Last Time>
Stella Blue>
Sugar Magnolia
*I Fought The Law
18 Songs

GARDEN OF THE GRATEFULLY DEADICATED
moves to its 4th location — Brazil!

Every $35 we raise will *permanently* protect one acre of endangered rainforest land in Brazil's Lagamar region. Through *DDN*, we Deadheads have raised over $24,000 to permanently preserve rainforest acreage. In addition, Bob Weir and Rob Wasserman recently did a benefit in Colorado where they raised almost $9,000, bringing our total to $33,000!!! We've been so successful that all the available land in our first three locations has been purchased through the Nature Conservancy's Adopt-An-Acre program.

Participate again or for the first time — send check or money order for any amount to: GARDEN OF THE GRATEFULLY DEADICATED, PO Box 148, Purdys, NY 10578

HEY NOW! CHECK OUT OUR NEW LOCATION...
IMPORTED CLOTHING & BACKPACKS • BEADED & GEMSTONE JEWELRY
T-SHIRTS & POSTERS & PINS
STICKERS & LIVE TAPE TRADING
PRIME CUTS
MUSIC EMPORIUM
LONG ISLAND'S
DEFINITIVE
DEAD QUARTERS
PROUD MEMBERS OF 1% FOR PEACE
516 678 0670
OUR BUSINESS IS DEAD & WE COULDN'T BE HAPPIER
191 N. LONG BEACH RD. ROCKVILLE CTR. N.Y. 11570
WE'RE BIGGER & BETTER & DEADER THAN EVER!!

DANCING BEAR GOODIES
OFFICIAL LICENSEE OF THE GRATEFUL DEAD

Send $1.00 for a new catalog to:

GRATEFUL GRAPHICS
4281 25th Street
San Francisco, CA 94114

Wholesale Inquiries Invited

Make your own TIE-DYES!
with...
Grateful Dyes

Bright...
Permanent...
FIBER REACTIVE DYES

c/o PIRATE RECORDS
2139 S. Sheridan Blvd.
Denver, CO 80227

303-763-8774

Send *SASE* for color & price list, or get started right away with our *Beginners Dye Kit* - 4 Colors & Instructions for just $20.50.
All orders come with complete instructions • Call for more information...

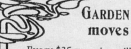

STILL GRATEFUL
AFTER ALL THESE YEARS

IN WHICH THE GRATEFUL DEAD, PINUP UGLIES OF THE HAIGHT-ASHBURY, BECOME THE HOUSE BAND OF THE AGE OF CERTAIN DOOM

BY CHARLIE HAAS

NEW ONES COMING AS THE OLD ONES GO

UYS IN THE traditional clown makeup and cardboard stars-and-stripes top hats; a circle of five grinning people gobbling sections of an orange fortified with vitamin LSD; skulls, skeletons and red roses on patches sewn to the breasts of denim jackets and the butts of denim pants; a girl in a garland of red roses like the one worn by the skeleton on the second live album and another girl in a baldy clown mask like the one worn by Garcia in the *Europe '72* photographs; and raiments silk-screened, heat-transferred and appliquéd with every known piece of Dead artwork, from the sperm-shooting skull on *Aoxomoxoa* to the fiddling fright-wigged skeleton on *Blues for Allah* to the skull-and-lightning-bolt on *Steal Your Face*; all of them wafting across the UCLA campus to Pauley Pavilion and most of them getting inside by 7, when the Dead secure the stage and start into "Jack Straw":

We can share the women,
We can share the wine . . .

Dawn of the Dead: *Above, the original cast (from left: Jerry Garcia, Bill Kreutzmann, Bob Weir, Phil Lesh, Ron "Pigpen" McKernan). At right, Garcia today.*

Shortly after this article was completed, Keith and Donna Godchaux retired from the Grateful Dead, and were replaced by keyboard player and tenor vocalist Brent Mydland.

Photographed by Herbie Greene

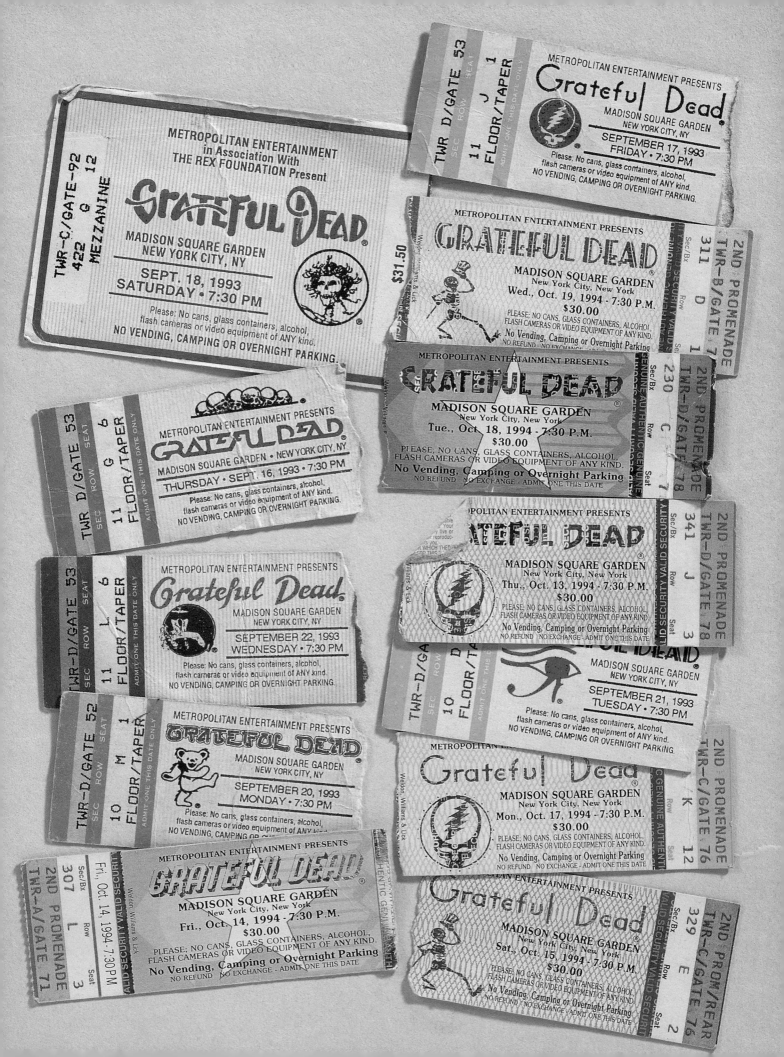

50-100

4/5/82 Phila. Spectrum
4/6/82 Phila. Spectrum
4/11/82 Nassau
4/12/82 Nassau
9/15/82 Landover, Md
9/20/82 Modison Square Garden
9/21/82 MSG
9/24/82 Carrier Dome, Syracuse, NY
4/14/83 Byrne Arena (w/Stephen Stills)
4/17/83 Byrne Arena (w/Stephen Stills)
4/25/83 Phila. Spectrum
6/20/83 Merriwether Post Pavilion
Columbia, MD

6/22/83 City Island, Harrisburg, PA.
9/6/83 Red Rocks Ampitheater
9/7/83 Morrison, Colorado
9/8/83

10/11/83 MSG
10/12/83 MSG
10/22/83 Carrier Dome, Syracuse

4/19/84 Civic Center
4/20/84 Philadelphia
4/21/84 Pennsylvania
6/23/84 City Island
6/24/84 Saratoga P.A.C, NY
10/17/84 Byrne Arena
10/18/84 Byrne Arena
10/20/84 Carrier Dome

3/28/85 Nassau
7/29/85 Nassau
4/6/85 Phila. Spectrum
4/7/85 Phila. Spectrum
4/3/85 Phila. Spectrum
6/21/85 Alpine Valley Music Theater
6/22/85 East Troy, Wisc.
6/23/85 Hershey Stadium, Hershey, PA
7/1/85 Merriwether Post Pavilion
11/1/85 Richmond Colliseum
11/2/85 Richmond, VA.
11/10/85 Byrne Arena
11/11/85 Byrne Arena
3/23/86 Phila. Spectrum
3/24/86 Phila. Spectrum
3/25/86 Phila. Spectrum
7/4/86 Rich Stadium, Orchard Park, NY
(hottest day → 7/7/86 R.F.K. Stadium, Washington, DC
ever - Jerry
collapses) 3/29/87 Phila. Spectrum
3/30/87 Phila. Spectrum
3/31/87 Phila. Spectrum
4/6/87 Byrne Arena
4/7/87 Byrne Arena

I like to move, to dance, to sway any way I want
I don't usually like to be crowded out of my seat
by people who don't want to sit in their own.
But I'll admit I couldn't stop help but
make an exception for the girl with
the flowers. When security cleared
the aisles, she squeezed in front of
me. And when the guard shined the
flashlight down our row, she moved in
close, like we were together. She
never turned around, but we swayed
together during "To Lay Me Down" or
"Peggy-O" or one of those songs, but
I don't remember which. As the first set
ended, she handed me her rose and left alone
before I could get myself together to speak
to her. I looked for her at nearly every
show I went to after that, and I
thought I saw her dozens of times.
Eventually, I knew that I'd never
know what she looked like —
she was an image in my head,
even while she stood there
But I had the rose.

Gene and I told Pit that he shouldn't come to the Hartford in March '90, because they were secret gigs—no mail order tickets, no out-of-state Ticketron—just local sales. Gene and I scored 2 tickets from his buddy, angle, who lived in Rhode Island. We told Pit these would be killer shows, because they were secret. We told Pit that too many people coming without tickets are ruining venues for the Dead. He knew that. Gene and I didn't have the heart to tell Pit he couldn't come. Pit had hope, and cash.

We drove up early in the morning just in case the box office saved tickets to sell on the day of the show. We walked around Hartford looking for the one person who had a ticket for Pit. In the middle of the afternoon, we split up to cover more territory. I had no luck and neither did Gene. But when we met back up Pit came running up, out of breath. He had just met Phil Lesh who was walking a baby carriage around with his son in it. Pit asked Phil if he had any extras. Phil laughed, Pit told us. Pit didn't find a ticket for that night but it didn't matter—he was still pumped when we met up with him after the show.

They Sang It :

"I've been all night coming home, don't eat cream cheese."
                                                    —Don Doe

"She had raisin hair, a ruffled dress, all the French perfume you care to smell."
                                                    —Gay the...

"The widow was so high on coke froze 10 feet 'neath the ground."
                                                    —Burns M°C

"Just a little pizza, just a little bite."
                                                    —Ness

"Askew, but straight in line."
                                                    —The roommate

"Sometimes we visit your beer tours and hang out at your zoos."
                                                    —Gore (7/11/81)

35,384,640 Tickets
1,272,090 Veggie Burritos
417,600 Hours of Music
92,878 Tie Dyes
3,812 VW Buses
644 Black Labs
30 Years
1 Band

GRATEFUL DEAD
1965 - 1995

The Official Sport of
Dead Tour

- Can be played with beer in hand
- Fits easily in your pocket
- Even a fool can play

Walk out of any doorway, feel your way, feel your way like the day before
Mayba you'll find direction

Somewhere around the corner where it's been waiting to meet you

What do you want me to do, to watch for you while you are sleeping?

Then please don't be surprised when you find me dreaming, too.

Cland
blows bubbles
to pass
the time

Cland likes the way
the bubbles float away
on the breeze

Ferd thought
that sounded like
fun. So he and
'd floated
'n

a LONG, STRANGE TRIP

"He was the leader of a band that was more than a band. It was a scene, it was a lifestyle."

—**Arnie Fagan,** 30, who sells T-shirts and other Grateful Dead memorabilia in his Cool Stuff store in Columbia, Mo.

JERRY GARCIA

Lead guitarist, composer and sometime vocalist for The Grateful Dead, a band that came to symbolize '60s counterculture, died yesterday of a heart attack.

■ ABOUT THE DEAD

■ Best-known songs: "Truckin'," "Casey Jones," "Friend of the Devil," "Touch of Grey," "Sugar Magnolia"

■ Became virtually a way of life to followers, known as "Dead-heads"

HA
the I

De
be a
bizar
high
the r
year,

In
relea
over
Beth
Stati
perc
large
Penn

St
fewe
viole
num
law
by

Jerry Garcia performs at a June 30 concert in Pittsburgh

Rock icon Jerry Garcia dies at 53

By JON PARELES
Of The New York Times

Jerry Garcia, 53, whose gentle voice and gleaming, chiming guitar lines embodied the psychedelic mellowness of the Grateful Dead for three decades, died in his sleep yesterday at Serenity Knolls, a residential drug treatment center in Forest Knolls, Calif.

A spokesman for the band, Dennis McNally, said the cause was a heart attack.

The guitarist had suffered serious health problems for a decade.

In the 1960s, he was known as "Captain Trips," referring to his frequent use of LSD, and he struggled through the years with heroin addiction.

He was hospitalized in 1986 in a diabetic coma, and in 1992 the group had to cancel tour dates when Garcia fell ill from exhaustion. In recent years, he had attempted to stop smoking and lose weight.

The Grateful Dead, and Garcia as their most recognizable member, had come to represent the survival of 1960s idealism. As news of his death spread, fans wept in the streets of San Francisco, and the In-

Please See **GARCIA** Page A14 ▶

Local fans remember star as a friend

By BOB LAYLO
Of The Morning Call

Frank Stancato will remember Jerry Garcia more for his friendliness than his guitar playing.

After a 1991 concert near Washington, D.C, Stancato, a Greenpeace activist, and some friends met the Grateful Dead guitarist at the Four Seasons Hotel in Baltimore. Garcia, who died yesterday, invited them to his suite.

Garcia stayed with his company until 6 a.m, talking about music, the Smithsonian

Please See **REACTION** Page A15 ▶

...his grandmother, who raised him, began a laundry workers union

■ Survived by his third wife and four daughters

■ Best known for his improvised guitar solos.

DEAD ON THE NET
Dead's newsletter on the Internet:

http://www.well.com/user/almanac

((o))

CALL INFO-TEL
Dial **821-8300**
or toll-free
1-800-879-6014;
categories can be dialed consecutively

■ For reaction of two **Deadheads** to death of **Grateful Dead** leader **Jerry Garcia,** enter categories **8860** and **8861**

■ **Hear a music clip** from Garcia and the band, category **8862**

■ **Reaction from rock critic Robert Cristgau,** writer for the Village Voice and Playboy, category **8863**

■ **General news updates** of Garcia's death enter categories **8684, 8698**

SOURCE: KRT

Copyright © 2001 by Scott Meyer

Printed in China

Library of Congress Cataloging-in-Publication Number 00 131325

ISBN-13: 978-0-7624-2836-6
ISBN-10: 0-7624-2836-8

Cover and interior design by Bill Jones
Edited by Molly Jay
Cover illustration by Bill Jones

This book may be ordered by mail from the publisher. Please add $2.50 for postage and handling. But try your bookstore first!

Published by Courage Books, an imprint of
Running Press Book Publishers
125 South Twenty-Second Street
Philadelphia, Pennsylvania 19103-4399
Visit us on the web!
www.runningpress.com